FOR MEN like Dr. Livingstone Africa was the "Dark Continent," sunk in ignorance and backwardness, awaiting only the rough grasp of the Europeans to shake it into life. These men knew nothing of the splendours of the African past. They saw only the tribal violence, which was partly caused by the coming of the European, and by the horrors of the slave trade. By the nineteenth century, the massive power of the industrial revolution enabled the white man to explore and divide the helpless continent; and fostered the belief in his racial superiority. Cecil Rhodes and other imperialists never dreamed there would be an end to their control of a passive and uncomplaining continent. But within eighty years, the fires of African nationalism and war had consumed them. The colonial era now seems only a brief episode in a great history stretching from Man's earliest settlements to the proud birth of independent states.

This book seeks to give a perspective to the history of Africa by seeing it through the eyes of numerous contemporaries, from explorers to missionaries, slaves to statesmen. Their letters, diaries and memoirs give us a fresh and vivid insight into the complex history of a remarkable continent, and into the lives of the men who experienced it.

The Making of Africa

Colin Nicolson

"The wind of change is blowing through this continent" –
Harold Macmillan, 1960.

WAYLAND PUBLISHERS · LONDON

G. P. PUTNAM'S SONS · NEW YORK

Frontispiece A Rhodesian mission school

SBN (hardback): 85340 288 4
Copyright © 1973 by Wayland (Publishers) Ltd
101 Grays Inn Road, London WC1
Set in 'Monophoto' Times and printed offset litho by
Page Bros (Norwich) Ltd, Norwich

Contents

The Illustrations

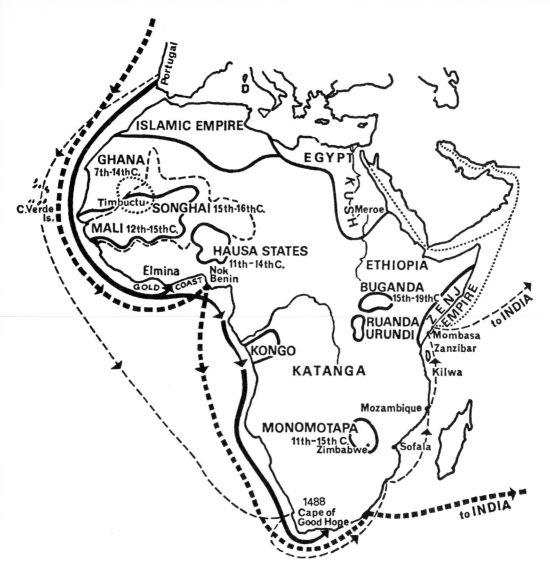

Empires and Kingdoms
approximate boundaries as far as known

Voyages of discovery & trade routes

➡ Bartholomew Diaz 1487-88
- - -➤ Vasco da Gama 1497-99
■■■➤ English Voyages 16th C
.... Trade routes to Arabia

The African continent: early empires and kingdoms; principal trade
routes and voyages of discovery

1 The African Past

"Dark Continent"

PERHAPS THE greatest mistake Europeans make about Africa is to believe that, before the coming of European man, Africa was a barbaric and uncivilized continent. They imagine it sunk in poverty, ignorance, witchcraft, cannibalism and tribal war, without history or culture. A governor of a British colony confirmed this view of the "Dark Continent": "They had no wheeled transport and . . . no animal transport either; they had no roads nor towns; no tools except the small hand hoes, axes, wooden digging sticks, and the like; no manufactures, and no industrial products except the simplest domestic handiwork; no commerce as we understand it and no currency, although in some places barter of produce was facilitated by the use of small shells; they had never heard of working for wages.

African life

"They went stark naked or clad in the bark of trees or the skins of animals; and they had no means of writing, even by hieroglyphics, nor of numbering except by their fingers or making notches in a stick or knots in a piece of grass or fibre; they had no weights or measures of general use. Perhaps most astonishing of all to the modern European mind they had no calendar nor notation of time. . .

"They were pagan, spirit or ancestor propitiators in the grip of magic or witchcraft, their minds cribbed and confined by superstition . . . They are a people who in 1890 were in a more primitive condition than anything of which there is any record in pre-Roman Britain (1)."

It was this view of Africa's past which eased the consciences of generations of slavers, plantation owners, and nineteenth century European conquerors. Of course savagery and brutality have been a part of African history. But they have been part of European history, too. Europeans have murdered, enslaved and tortured millions of their fellow men.

Africa's past   However, most Europeans did not know that Africa had been the centre of rich and splendid civilizations many centuries before the first European travellers arrived in their crude wooden ships. It is now accepted that the splendours of Ancient Egypt are as much part of the history of Africa as they are of the Middle East. Many of the Pharaohs were Africans. The impact of the states they ruled was extended throughout the continent by military campaigns, merchants and travellers.

Ancient Egypt   Around 2300 B.C. the Egyptian Harkuf led four expeditions deep into the interior: "I went forth," reads the inscription on his tomb, "upon the [Aswan] road, and I descended from Irthet, Mekher, Tereres, Irtheth, being an affair of eight months. When I descended I brought gifts from this country in very great quantity. Never before was the like brought to this land (2)."

Meroë   When Egypt's power began to decline in the fifth century B.C. the centre of power shifted southward to the city of Meroë, in what is now the Sudan. This brought the civilization of Egypt even more deeply into the African continent. For more than seven centuries Meroë flourished, becoming the centre of an iron industry which a modern archaeologist described as "the Birmingham of Central Africa."

Centuries later, the ruins of the city were still recognizable. James Bruce, the eighteenth-century Scottish traveller, noted the remains of "heaps of broken pedestals, like those of Axum, . . . some pieces of obelisk, likewise, with hieroglyphics, almost totally obliterated. The Arabs told us these ruins were very extensive; and that many pieces of statues, both of men and animals, had been dug up there; the statues of the men were mostly of black stone. It is impossible to avoid risking a guess that this is the ancient city of Meroë . . . (3)"

Rome and Africa   Later, when the Romans controlled the Mediterranean coast of Africa, they had much contact with African communities south of the Sahara, but made no attempt to conquer them. For the Romans, the interior of Africa remained almost unknown.

But it did supply wild beasts and gladiators for the public *Wild animals*
games. One Sicilian mosaic shows mounted men "driving stags
into a circle of nets, one stag having already been caught by his
antlers. Another shows men loading elephants onto a galley
while others drag an unwilling rhino calf toward the gang-plank
as trained dogs snap at the animal from the rear. Still others
show a Roman animal catcher with a huge shield pointing to a
lion who is eating an oryx he has just killed. . .

"Organizing these hunts must have been a tremendous undertaking. The catchers could demand that legionnaires stationed
in their area help with the drives; and the commanders had to
co-operate, for getting the animals was crucial to the politicians
in Rome. The whole civilian population could be drafted for
this work and, as some of Cicero's angry letters show, this often
crippled the local economy, for many of these drives lasted for
weeks (4)."

Such exploitation was in later centuries, too, to characterize
the life of the people of Africa.

The Kingdoms of the Sahara

In A.D. 639 the Muslim Arabs invaded Egypt. By the beginning *Muslim*
of the next century they were masters of the whole North African *invasions*
coast, from Alexandria to the Atlantic, and were threatening to
sweep into Europe itself. These Muslim conquests were of
enormous importance to Africa, for the cultural unity which
Islam imposed on its conquered territories lasted for centuries.
There arose from the conquest a sophisticated civilization with
a highly developed administrative and legal system. But, above
all, the Muslim conquest brought order and peace. So trade and
learning flourished, and men could travel without fear. Arab
scholars and travellers like Al Bekri, Al Omari and Ibn Battuta,
were among the first to visit Africa south of the Sahara – an
area which had so long been shrouded in mystery.

It is clear from these travellers' accounts that, in the early *Powerful*
Middle Ages, there were states in the western Sudan which were *African states*
equal to those in contemporary Europe. In 1067, only a year

The rich trading city of Timbuctu, drawn by an early French traveller

after William of Normandy conquered England, Al Bekri, the Arab writer, visited Ghana. His description shows just how powerful the country was, for the king could "put two hundred thousand warriors in the field, more than forty thousand being armed with bow and arrow.

"When he gives an audience to his people, to listen to their complaints and set them to rights, he sits in a pavilion around which stand ten pages holding shields and gold-mounted swords: and on his right hand are the sons of the princes of his empire, splendidly clad and with gold plaited into their hair.

The governor of the city is seated on the ground in front of the King, and all around him are his vizirs in the same position. The gate of the chamber is guarded by dogs of an excellent breed, who never leave the King's seat: they wear collars of gold and silver, ornamented with the same metals (5)."

Lying across the profitable trade routes which exchanged the gold of West Africa for the salt of the Sahara, medieval Ghana became a rich and powerful state, well known to European rulers of the time, like the Norman king, Roger II of Sicily. In the mid-thirteenth century Ghana was superseded by an even more powerful state, Mali. Under a succession of strong rulers, Mali enjoyed a period of great prosperity. The wealth of the trans-Sahara trade gave rise to rich towns; Djenné, Kumbi, and, above all, Timbuctu, became renowned as centres of learning and scholarship. *Ghana*

A sixteenth-century writer vividly described Timbuctu: "Here are shops of artificers and merchants, and especially of such as weave linen and cotton cloth. And hither do the Barbary merchants bring cloth of Europe. All the women of this region, except the maidservants, go with their faces covered, and sell all necessary victuals. The inhabitants, and especially strangers there residing, are exceeding rich, insomuch that the King that now is, married both his daughters to rich merchants. Here are many wells containing most sweet water; and so often as the River Niger overfloweth, they convey the water thereof by certain sluices into the town. *Prosperous cities*

"Corn, cattle milk, and butter this region yieldeth in great abundance: but salt is very scarce there . . .

"The rich King of Timbuktu hath many plates and sceptres of gold, some whereof weigh 1,300 pounds: and he keeps a magnificent and well-furnished court . . . Here are great store of doctors, judges, priests, and other learned men, that are bountifully maintained at the King's cost and charges, and hither are brought divers manuscripts or written books out of Barbary, which are sold for more money than any other merchandise. The coin of Timbuktu is of gold without any stamp or superscription: but in matters of small value they use certain shells brought hither out of the kingdom of Persia . . . (6)" *Timbuctu*

Mansa Musa   The greatest of the rulers of Mali was the warrior King Mansa Musa, who was renowned for the great wealth and splendour of his court. Al Omari describes the devastating effect of the King's visit to Egypt in 1324, *en route* to Mecca: "This man [Mansa Musa] . . . spread upon Cairo the flood of his generosity: there was no person, officer of the [Cairo] court or holder of any office of the [Cairo] sultanate who did not receive a sum in gold from him. The people of Cairo earned incalculable sums from him, whether by buying and selling or by gifts. So much gold was current in Cairo that it ruined the value of money! . . .

"Let me add," Omari goes on, "that gold in Egypt had enjoyed a high rate of exchange up to the moment of their arrival. The gold mitqual that year had fallen below twenty-five drachmas. But from that day [of their arrival] onward, its value dwindled; the exchange was ruined, and even now it has not recovered. The mitqual scarcely touches twenty-two drachmas. That is how it has been for twelve years from that time, because of the great amounts of gold they brought to Egypt and spent there (7)."

Ibn Battuta   Perhaps the most fascinating of all the Arab travellers to visit the medieval African states was Muhammad Ibn Abdulah Ibn Battuta. A native of Marrakesh, he spent most of his life on a series of expeditions. Among the countries he visited in the Muslim world were India, Persia, Africa, Russia and even China.

Mali   In 1352 Ibn Battuta crossed the Sahara to visit the renowned kingdom of Mali. He recounted some of the splendours he saw: "On certain days the sultan holds audiences in the palace yard, where there is a platform under a tree, with three steps; this they call the pempi. It is carpeted with silk and has cushions place on it. [Over it] is raised the umbrella, which is a sort of pavillion made of silk, surmounted by a bird in gold, about the size of a falcon. The sultan comes out of a door in a corner of the palace, carrying a bow in his hand and a quiver on his back. On his head he has a golden skullcap, bound with a gold band which has narrow ends shaped like knives, more than a span in length. His usual dress is a velvety red tunic, made of the European fabrics called mutanfas.

"The sultan is preceded by his musicians, who carry gold and silver guimbris [two-stringed guitars], and behind him come three hundred armed slaves . . . On reaching the pempi he stops and looks round the assembly . . . As he takes his seat the drums, trumpets, and bugles are sounded (8)."

Like many subsequent visitors, Ibn Battuta found certain African customs disconcerting. "These people," he complained, "have some deplorable customs . . . Women servants, slave women and young girls go about quite naked, not even concealing their sexual parts. I saw many like this during Ramadhan; because it is the custom with the Negroes that commanding officers should break their fast in the Sultan's palace, and they are served with food which is brought by women slaves, twenty or more of them who are completely naked.

African customs

"Women go naked into the Sultan's presence, too, without even a veil; his daughters also go about naked. On the twenty-seventh night of Ramadhan I saw about a hundred women slaves coming out of the Sultan's palace with food, and they were naked. Two daughters of the Sultan were with them, and these had no veil either, although they had big breasts (9)."

But, on the whole, Battuta approved of African manners: "Among the admirable qualities of these people," he wrote, "the following are to be noted. The small numbers of acts of injustice that one finds there; for the Negroes are of all peoples those who most abhor injustice. The Sultan pardons no one who is guilty of it. The complete and general safety one enjoys throughout the land. The traveller has no more reason than the man who stays at home to fear brigands, thieves or ravishers. The blacks do not confiscate the goods of white men [North Africans] who die in their country, not even when these consist of big treasures. They deposit them, on the contrary, with a man of confidence among the whites until those who have a right to the goods present themselves and take possession (10)."

The reports of these travellers clearly show that some states in Africa were possibly more advanced than those of medieval Europe. The rulers of Ghana, Mali and Songhai, which eventually eclipsed Mali, controlled wealthy ordered societies, in which trade flourished and men could lead peaceful lives within the walls of fine cities like Timbuctu and Kimbu.

Early East Africa

Medieval
Mombasa

In 1331 the famous traveller Ibn Battuta, sailed from Aden for the eastern coast of Africa, to visit the great trading port of Kilwa. "We arrived at Mombasa," he wrote, "a large island two days' journey from the land of the Swahili. The island is quite separate from the mainland. It grows bananas, lemons, and oranges . . . The people do not engage in agriculture, but import grain from the Swahili . . .

"We spent a night on the Island [of Mombasa] and then set sail for Kilwa, the principal town on the coast, the greater part of whose inhabitants are Zenj of very black complexion. Their faces are scarred, like the Limiin of Janada. A merchant told me that Sofala is half a month's march . . . Powdered gold is brought from Yufi to Sofala.

Kilwa

"Kilwa is one of the most beautiful and well-constructed towns in the world. The whole of it is elegantly built. The roofs are built with mangrove poles. There is very much rain (11)."

Zenj Empire

Kilwa was in the Empire of the Zenj – an area that had grown up from the numerous trading cities strung along the African shore of the Indian Ocean. It was perhaps the richest, as well as the oldest, civilization existing in medieval Africa. The Chinese knew of it as early as 202 B.C., and, about A.D. 1100, a Chinese visitor recorded: "The country of Po-pa-li is in the south-western area. [The people] do not eat any of the five grains but eat only meat. They often stick a needle into the veins of cattle and draw blood, which they drink raw, mixed with milk . . . From olden times on they were not subject to any foreign country. In fighting they use elephants' tusks and ribs and the horns of wild buffaloes as lances, and they wear cuirasses and bows and arrows. They have twenty myriads of foot soldiers. The Arabs make frequent raids on them (12)."

Ivory trade

When Ibn Battuta visited the Zenj Empire in the fourteenth century, it was part of a rich commercial network linking India, Ceylon, China and Arabia. African ivory sold well throughout

Opposite Vasco da Gama, one of the first European explorers to sail round the southernmost tip of Africa – the Cape of Good Hope

Asia, as an Arab visitor, Al Masudi, explained: "In China the kings and their military and civilian officers used carrying-chairs of ivory; no official or person of rank would dare to visit the king in an iron chair, and ivory alone is used for this purpose. . . Ivory is much prized in India: there it is made into handles for the daggers known as harari, or harri in the singular, as well as for the hilts of curved swords . . . But the biggest use of ivory is in the manufacture of chessmen and other gaming pieces (13)."

Vasco da Gama

In 1497 the Portuguese sea-captain, Vasco da Gama, forced his unwilling crew past the barrier which had prevented Europeans from reaching India: they rounded Cape of Good Hope. Struggling up the deserted coast of south-east Africa, seeing only a few primitive Hottentots, da Gama was about to continue his journey eastwards towards India, when he came upon the rich and unknown Empire of Zenj. His astonished crew sailed past city after city, each rivalling the next in the splendour of its buildings, the wealth of its inhabitants, and the number of trading vessels thronging its harbours.

Prosperous townsmen

But the inhabitants were not impressed by da Gama and his cheap trading goods. "When we had been two or three days at this place," da Gama wrote in his log, "two gentlemen of the country came to see us. They were very haughty, and valued nothing which we gave them. One of them wore a touca, with a fringe embroidered in silk, and the other a cap of green satin. A young man in their company – so we understood from their signs – had come from a distant country, and had already seen big ships like ours. These tokens gladdened our hearts, for it appeared as if we were really approaching the bourne of our desires (14)."

Da Gama soon had more opportunities to study these people and their cities. There is, perhaps, an ominous note of greed in this entry: "The people of this country," he wrote in his log book several days later, "are of a ruddy complexion and well made. They are Mohammedans, and their language is the same as that of the Moors. Their dresses are of fine linen or cotton stuffs, with variously coloured stripes, and of rich and elaborate workmanship. They all wear toucas with borders of silk embroidered in gold.

18

Trade and barter brought the first contacts between Europeans and the peoples of the African continent

"They are merchants, and have transactions with white Moors [Indians], four of whose vessels were at the time in port, laden with gold, silver, cloves, pepper, ginger, and silver rings, as also with quantities of pearls, jewels, and rubies, all of which articles are used by the people of this country (15)." *Zenj merchants*

He took a professional interest in the ships of the Zenj, noting with surprise that "their mariners have Genoese needles, by which they steer, quadrants, and navigating charts (16)." Such navigational aids had been used for centuries on the Indian Ocean. *Navigational aids*

A few years later another Portuguese traveller, Duarte Barbosa, a commercial agent of the King, visited the east coast.

19

His is the last description of the Zenj cities before the depredations of the Europeans shattered the balance of trade in the Indian Ocean and caused the decline of the cities. Barbosa visited the greatest of them, Kilwa. It was, he wrote, a town "with many fair houses of stone and mortar, with many windows after our fashion, very well arranged in streets, with many flat roofs. The doors are of wood, well carved, with excellent joinery. Around it are streams and orchards and fruit-gardens with many channels of sweet water. It has a Moorish King over it.

The gold trade   "From this place," he continued, "they trade with Sofala, whence they bring back gold . . . And in this town was great plenty of gold, as no ships passed towards Sofala without first coming to this island.

"Of the Moors there are some fair and some black, they are finely clad in many rich garments of gold and silk and cotton, and the women as well; also with much gold and silver in chains and bracelets, which they wear on their legs and arms, and many jewelled earrings in their ears (17)."

Mombasa   Barbosa also described Mombasa: "Along the coast towards India, there is an isle hard by the mainland, on which is a town called Mombasa. It is a very fair place, with lofty stone and mortar houses, well aligned in streets after the fashion of Kilwa. The wood is well fitted with excellent joiner's work. It has its own King, himself a Moor. The men are in colour either tawny, black or white and also their women go very bravely [finely] attired with many fine garments of silk and gold in abundance."

Mombasa's trade   He continues, in the tone of an experienced commercial agent: "This is a place of great traffic, and has a good harbour, in which are always moored craft of many kinds and also great ships, both of those which come from Sofala and those which go thither, and others which come from the great kingdom of Cambay and from Malindi; others which sail to the Isles of Zanzibar, and yet others of which I shall speak anon (18)."

Barbosa found a great variety of food in Mombasa: "There are found many very fine sheep with round tails, cows and other cattle in great plenty, and many fowls, all of which are exceeding fat. There is much millet and rice, sweet and bitter oranges, lemons, pomegranates, Indian figs, vegetables of divers kinds,

20

and much sweet water. The men . . . carry on trade with them, bringing thence great store of honey, wax and ivory (19)."

It was the quantity of gold everywhere that really excited the *Greed for gold* early visitors. Was there, the Portuguese asked themselves, another Mexico somewhere in the mysterious interior? Driven by curiosity and greed, many ignored the dangers of the unknown and pushed slowly inland. They did not discover another fabulous place like El Dorado, but their accounts reveal the existence of another important civilization in what is now Rhodesia and Mozambique. Modern archaeologists have made amazing discoveries in this part of Africa. Huge and ancient stone structures rise in the bush; hundreds of mine-shafts exist, sunk many centuries before European prospectors arrived. This was the civilization of Monomotapa and Zimbabwe.

A sixteenth-century explorer described his finds in medieval *Medieval* Rhodesia: "These mines are all in the plain, in the midst of *mines* which there is a square fortress, of masonry within and without, built of stones of marvellous size, and there appears to be no mortar joining them. The wall is more than twenty-five spans in width, and the height is not so great considering the width. Above the door of this edifice is an inscription, which some Moorish merchants, learned men, who went thither, could not read, neither could they tell what the character might be.

"This edifice is almost surrounded by hills, upon which are others resembling it in the fashioning of the stone and the absence of mortar, and one of them is a tower more than twelve fathoms high . . . When, and by whom these edifices were raised, as the people of the land are ignorant of the art of writing, there is no record, but they say they are the work of the devil, for in comparison with their power and knowledge it does not seem possible to them that they should be the work of man (20)."

As our knowledge of Africa expands, it becomes clear that *African history* far from being a "Dark Continent" sunk in simplicity and savagery, Africa had a long and complex history. Ancient Egypt, Carthage and Rome, the great civilizations of China and of medieval Islam, had all influenced Africa's growth. While Europeans were plunged in medieval feuds and religious wars,

The fifteenth-century European view of Africa: a map drawn by
Christopher Columbus's pilot

the kingdoms of Ghana, Mali, and Songhai were enjoying
prosperity and peace, and the ships of the Zenj pursued a trade
which spanned the Indian Ocean and touched the Pacific.
While Europeans burned witches, slaughtered heretics and
waged "holy wars" of terrible ferocity, the Hottentots of
southern Africa led simpler, but hardly inferior lives. A Swedish
traveller described their existence, unchanged for centuries:
"The Hottentots who live in these parts, . . . seldom make use

22

of any weapons. Here and there, indeed, a man will furnish himself with a javelin, by way of defence against the wolves: this is called a hassagai.

"Their habitations are as simple as their dress, and equally adapted to the wandering pastoral life they lead in those parts. In fact, they scarcely merit any other name than that of huts; though not, perhaps, as spacious and eligible as the tents and dwelling-places of the patriarchs, at least they are sufficient for the Hottentot's wants and desires. He may therefore be considered as a happy man, in being able in this point likewise so easily to satisfy them.

"The great simplicity of them is, perhaps, the reason, why in a Hottentot's craal, or village, the huts are all built exactly alike; and that one meets there with a species of architecture, that does not a little contribute to keep envy from insinuating itself under their roofs (21)."

But, by the end of the fifteenth century, Europe was beginning to reach out towards Africa for the first time; the contact between the two continents was to have profound consequences for both of them.

Hottentots

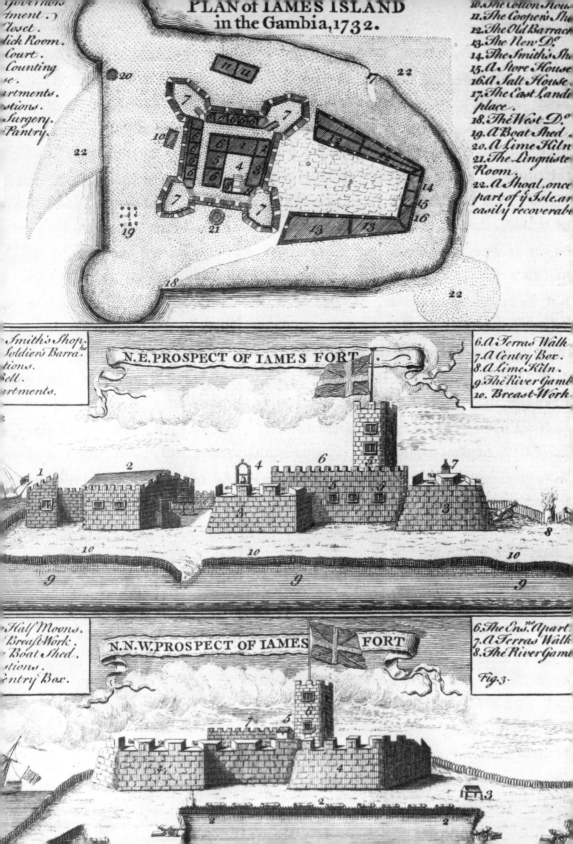

PLAN of IAMES ISLAND
in the Gambia, 1732.

Governors
ment.
Closet.
lick Room.
Court.
Counting
se.
rtments.
tions.
Surgery.
Pantry.

10. The Cotton Hous.
11. The Cooper's Sh.
12. The Old Barrac
13. The New D.º
14. The Smith's Sh.
15. A Store House.
16. A Salt House.
17. The East Land
place.
18. The West D.º
19. A Boat Shed.
20. A Lime Kiln.
21. The Linguiste
Room.
22. A Shoal, once
part of ƴ Isle, ar
easily recoverab

Smith's Shop.
Soldiers Barra
tions.
ell.
rtments.

N.E. PROSPECT OF IAMES FORT

6. A Terras Walk
7. A Centry Box.
8. A Lime Kiln.
9. The River Gamb
10. Breast-Work

Half Moons.
Breast Work.
Boat Shed.
tions.
entry Box.

N.N.W. PROSPECT OF IAMES FORT

6. The Ens.ᵗˢ Apart
7. A Terras Walk
8. The River Gamb

Fig. 3.

2 The Slave Centuries

WITH THE coming of Europeans the history of Africa entered a *New* new phase. As we have seen, there was little difference between *navigational* the development of Europe and Africa in the fifteenth century. *aids* But in that century European sailors, using the new navigation aids, like the lateen sail, the astrolabe, and the compass, began to sail further than ever before. In the half century after 1434, the Portuguese rounded the Cape of Good Hope and entered the Indian Ocean. The consequences for Europe and Africa were far-reaching.

Within a few years of da Gama's discovery of the Zenj *Portuguese* Empire, the Portuguese, enflamed by religious zeal and greed *raids* for gold, started to raid the trading cities of the coast.

Duarte Barbosa, the King's agent, noted contemptuously that, despite their obvious luxury and wealth, the inhabitants "are feeble folk, and have but few weapons." A scholar in Kilwa recognized the danger posed by the newcomers. "Those who know the truth," he wrote, "confirmed that they were corrupt and dishonest persons who had only come to spy out the land in order to destroy it (22)." Within a few years his judgement was proved only too correct.

The Portuguese attacked Mombasa. A German merchant *Sack of* described what happened: "The Grand-Captain ordered that *Mombasa* the town should be sacked and that each man should carry off to his ship whatever he found: so that at the end there would be a division of the spoil, each man to receive a twentieth of what he found. The same rule was made for gold, silver and pearls.

25

Opposite European countries controlled the slave trade from forts such as this one, built along the coast of West Africa

Then everyone started to plunder the town and to search the houses, forcing open doors with axes and iron bars (23)."

Brava destroyed   A similar fate befell the city of Brava: "Yet further along the coast, beyond these places, is a great town of Moors, of very fine stone and mortar houses, called Brava . . . And this place was destroyed by the Portuguese, who slew many of its people and carried many into captivity, and took great spoil of gold and silver and goods. Thenceforth many of them fled away towards the inland country, forsaking the town; yet after it had been destroyed the Portuguese again settled and peopled it, so that now it is as prosperous as it was before (24)."

Within a short time the Portuguese had destroyed or subjugated all the old and splendid cities of Zenj. But, not content with taking the cities of the coast, the greed of the Portuguese made them press inland, seeking for the gold mines of the Monomotapa.

Monomotapa's humiliation   In 1607 they forced this humiliating document upon a once proud and independent monarch: "I, the Emperor Monomotapa, think fit and am pleased to give to his Majesty all the mines of gold, copper, iron, lead, and pewter which may be in my empire, so long as the King of Portugal, to whom I give the said mines, shall maintain me in my position (25)."

Portuguese in West Africa   In West Africa the Portuguese impact was less obviously destructive. They intended to trade and convert the inhabitants to Christianity. To help spread the Christian faith, King John II of Portugal "sent holy and most catholic advisers with praiseworthy admonitions for the faith to administer a stern rebuke about the heresies and great idolatries and fetishes, which the Negroes practice in that land (26)."

Castle building   To carry on their missionary and trading activities the Europeans needed a base on the coast. But the difficulties of finding adequate building materials were immense. King John proposed a bold solution: "he ordered that all the timber and freestones, which would be necessary for the gates, the windows, the corner-rafters of the walls, the tower, and other things, should forthwith be cut and shaped in this country, so that without any delay in the work they could be set in place immediately (27)."

So the Portuguese were able to build a great castle. They *The Castle of* called it the Castle of the Mine, because they were convinced *the Mine* they would discover in West Africa gold mines as big as those in Mexico.

The Portuguese did not, however, control the African trade *Trade rivals* for long. As the sixteenth century progressed, English, French, Dutch, and even Danes and Brandenburgers (from the state of Brandenburg in Germany) challenged the Portuguese monopoly, trading textiles and hardware for the gold, pepper and ivory which West Africa supplied so abundantly. It was a profitable trade, with advantages for both sides; and the Africans were certainly not exploited.

John Lok, the English trader, found the Africans "very wary *Hard* people in their bargaining, and will not lose one sparke of golde *bargaining* of any value. They use weights and measures, and are very circumspect in occupying the same. They that shall have to doe with them, must use them gently; for they will not traffick or bring in any wares, if they be evil used (28)."

Many years later a Dutch trader, Bosman, complained that *Misunder-* many people in Europe were convinced that white men con- *standings* trolled and dominated the commerce with Africa. They believed, he said, "that the Gold Mines are in our power; that we, like the Spaniards in the West Indies, have no more to do but to work them by our slaves: though you perfectly know we have no manner of access to these treasures. Nor do I believe that any of our people have ever seen one of them. This you will easily credit, when you are informed that the negroes esteem them sacred, and consequently take all possible care to keep us from them (29)."

Unfortunately the trade between Africa and Europe was not *The slave* to remain on such an equal footing. As early as 1441 ten Africans *trade begins* were taken from their homes and sent as gifts to Prince Henry the Navigator. In 1444 another 235 men, women and children were brought from Africa to be sold as household servants in Portugal. This was the beginning of the trade which would eventually poison relations between Africa and Europe. Forts like the Castle of the Mine ceased to be centres of peaceful trad-

The slave trade to America brought prosperity to Liverpool, shown here,
and many other English ports

ing. Instead they became staging posts in a corrupt and humiliating traffic in human flesh. The slave trade had begun.

Slaves for sale   A conversation between an African trader and the Englishman, Richard Jobson, at the beginning of the seventeenth century, illustrates early feelings about slave trading. The trader had offered to sell Jobson several Negro girls as slaves: "I made answer," he writes, "we were a people who did not deal in any such commodities, neither did we buy or sell one another, or any that had our own shapes. He seemed to marvel much at it, and told me it was the only merchandise they carried down into the country, where they fetch all their salt, and that they were sold there to white men who earnestly desired them (30)."

The Spanish and Portuguese colonies in South America needed a constant supply of labour for their plantations and mines. From the mid-seventeenth century the development of the West Indian sugar colonies increased the demands for slaves still further. In towns like Liverpool, Amsterdam and Nantes merchants grew rich on the proceeds of the "triangular trade" – the trade in manufactures for Africa, slaves for the new world colonies, and sugar, tobacco and spices for the old world.

Demand for slaves

But what of the Africans, without whom the trade could not have existed?

Slavery in Africa

Firstly, slavery existed in Africa before the arrival of the Europeans. The people sold to Europeans were often already household slaves or prisoners of war. As the Dutch merchant, Bosman, explained to a friend: "Not a few in our country fondly imagine that parents here sell their children, men their wives, and one brother the other. But those who think so deceive themselves, for this never happens on any other account but that of necessity, or some great crime. But most of the slaves that are offered to us are prisoners of war, which are sold by the victors as their booty (31)."

Indeed African wars were very much to the advantage of European slavers. According to Bosman: "The Gold Coast, in times of war between the inland nations, and those nearer the sea, will furnish great numbers of slaves of all sexes and ages; sometimes at one place, and sometimes at another, as has been already observed, according to the nature of the war, and the situation of the countries between which it is waged. I remember, to this purpose that in the year 1681, an English interloper at Commenda got three hundred good slaves, almost for nothing

Prisoners of war

besides the trouble of receiving them at the beach in his boats . . . (32)"

In fact, if conditions were peaceful, Europeans could find business difficult: "At other times slaves are so scarce there," complained Bosman, "that in 1682 I could get but eight from one end of the coast to the other . . . by reason the natives were everywhere at peace (33)."

Trade goods
It was usual for African chiefs and headmen to sell captives and domestic slaves to the European slavers. Each slaver tried to outdo the others, tempting the kings and chiefs with their trade goods. The English, we are told, "have tapseils broad and narrow, nicanees fine and coarse; many sorts of chints, or Indian calicoes: printed, tallow, red painting colours; Canary wines, sayes, perpetuanas, inferior to the Dutch, and sack'd up in painted tillets, with the English arms: many sorts of white calicoes; blue and white linen, China satins, Barbadoes rum, or *aqua-vitae*, made from sugar, other strong waters . . . (34)"

Crooked businessmen
As slave-trading began to dominate all other business, Africans became crafty businessmen and drove hard bargains: "since they have so often been imposed upon by the Europeans, who in former ages made no scruple to cheat them in the qualities, weight and measure of their goods (35)."

Soon, straight-forward trading and barter was quite inadequate to meet the insatiable demands of the slave-ships crowding the ports. Captains were forced to offer gold to obtain captives. "Gold commands the trade," complained an Englishman in 1771. "There is no buying a slave without one ounce of gold upon it (36)."

Hard bargainers
Some kings made full use of the shortage to drive merciless bargains. "But before we can deal with any person," laments the Dutchman Bosman, "we are obliged to buy the King's whole stock of slaves at a set price; which is commonly one third or one fourth higher than ordinary (37)."

Kidnap victims
The dearth of victims inevitably tempted unscrupulous dealers to kidnap peaceful Africans, and forcibly carry them into slavery. This was quite easy, because the Africans were so unsuspicious. One Spanish captain found that: "The condition of these natives, when they feed themselves on fish alone, is

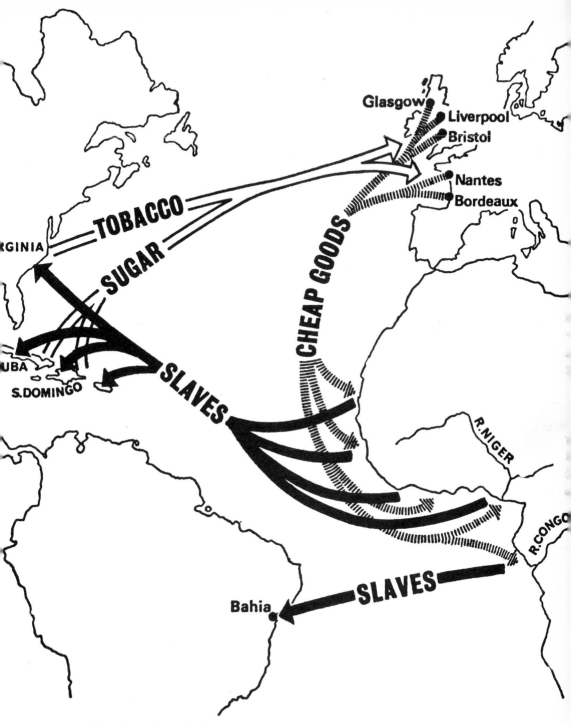

The "triangular trade" between Europe, Africa and America

very gentle, and as they always walk unarmed by the lagoons, they suffer themselves to be seized without difficulty by warlike and unarmed men (38)." A cheap and easy way to get slaves.

Revenge   However, unscrupulous slavers did not always have it their own way. One contemporary writer describes how the "captain of an English ship, which had been some time in that river, had enticed several of the natives on board, and, finding a favourable opportunity, sailed away with them. His vessel however was . . . driven back to the coast . . . and was obliged to cast anchor on the very spot where this act of treachery had been committed.

"At this time two other English vessels were lying in the same river. The natives, ever since the transaction, had determined to retaliate . . . They accordingly boarded the three vessels, and, having made themselves masters of them, they killed most of their crews. The few who escaped to tell the tale, were obliged to take refuge in a neighbouring French factory. Thus did the innocent suffer the same punishment as the guilty; for it did not appear that the crews of the other two vessels had been at all concerned in this villainous measure (39)."

Before examining the consequences of the trade and the part it played in the development of Africa, we must understand the fate of the trade's victims.

Frightened   The English explorer Mungo Park, who wrote late in the
slaves   eighteenth century, spoke to a group of fearful slaves awaiting the dreaded journey to the coast. "Eleven of them confessed to me that they had been slaves from their infancy; but the other two refused to give any account of their former condition. They were all very inquisitive; but they viewed me at first with looks of horror, and repeatedly asked if my countrymen were cannibals. They were very desirous to know what became of the slaves after they had crossed the salt water. I told them that they were employed in cultivating the land, but they would not believe me . . .

"A deeply rooted idea that the whites purchase Negroes for the purpose of devouring them, or of selling them to others, that they may be devoured hereafter, naturally makes the slaves
Fettered   contemplate a journey towards the coast with great terror . . .
32   *slaves*   "They are commonly secured [in irons] by putting the right

leg of one and the left of another into the same pair of fetters. By supporting the fetters with a string, they can walk, though very slowly. Every four slaves are likewise fastened together by the necks with a strong rope or twisted thongs; and in the night an additional pair of fetters is put on their hands, and sometimes a light iron chain passed round their necks (40)."

If the slaves were troublesome, other steps were taken. "A thick billet of wood is cut about three feet long, and a smooth notch being made upon one side of it, the ankle of the slave is bolted to the smooth part by means of a strong iron staple, one prong of which passes on each side of the ankle. All these fetters and bolts are made from native iron (41)."

The journey to the coast was one of frightful hardship and suffering. Those who could not make it were shot by the overseers or left to die of starvation and thirst in the bush. The others were forced on, threatened by the guns and whips of their captors.

Terrible journey

William Bosman, the Dutchman, described the treatment of the captives when they reached the coast. "When these slaves come to Fida," he wrote, "they are put in prison all together, and when we treat concerning buying them, they are all brought out together in a large plain . . . Here they are thoroughly examined . . .

"Those which are approved as good are set on one side; and the lame or faulty are set by as invalids, which are here called mackrons. These are such as are above five and thirty years old, or are maimed in the arms, legs, hands or feet, have lost a tooth, are grey-haired, or have films over their eyes; as well as all those which are affected with any venereal distemper, or with several other diseases.

Examination of slaves

"The invalids and the maimed being thrown out . . . the remainder are numbered, and it is entered who delivered them. In the meanwhile a burning iron, with the arms or name of the companies, lies in the fire; with which ours are marked on the breast.

Branding

"I doubt not but this trade seems very barbarous to you . . . but we yet take all possible care that they are not burned too hard, especially the women, who are more tender than the

33

Overleaf Sailors chaining slaves together as they take them on board a European slave ship

men (42)."

Once loaded aboard the slave-ships these men, women and
children ceased to be part of the history of Africa. Instead they
became tragic, stateless figures, caught in the vicious systems
of contemporary agriculture and social attitudes. The "middle
passage," the voyage to America, was horrifying. The terrible
conditions in which the slaves travelled were only equalled by
the brutal treatment they received from the ships' crews.

A British surgeon described conditions on a typical slave
vessel: "Some wet and blowing weather," he writes, "having
occasioned the port-holes to be shut, and the grating to be
covered, fluxes and fevers among the negroes ensued. While
they were in this situation, my profession requiring it, I frequently
went down among them, till at length their apartments became
so extremely hot as to be only sufferable for a short time.

"But," he continues, "the excessive heat was not the only
thing that rendered their situation intolerable. The deck, that is
the floor of their rooms, was so covered with the blood and
mucous which had proceeded from them in consequence of the
flux [dysentery], that it resembled a slaughter-house. It is not in
the power of the human imagination to picture to itself a situation more dreadful or disgusting. Numbers of the slaves having
fainted, they were carried up on deck, where several of them died
and the rest were, with great difficulty, restored. It had nearly
proved fatal to me also (43)."

An African, Ottobah Cuguano, one of the few slaves to gain
his freedom, gave a vivid impression of his feelings when he was
put on board ship at Cape Coast Castle. "There was nothing
to be heard but the rattling of chains, smacking of whips, and
the groans and cries of our fellow-men. Some would not stir
from the ground, when they were lashed and beat in the most
horrible manner ... When we were put into the ship we saw
several black merchants coming on board, but we were all drove
into our holes and not suffered to speak to any of them. In this
situation we continued several days in sight of our native
land (44)."

For more than 400 years the slave trade dominated the
relationship between Africans and Europeans. The promising

early contacts based upon trade were destroyed, first by Portuguese greed in the Indian Ocean, and later by the evils of the slave trade. It has been estimated that Africa lost between thirty and forty million people through the slave trade. How did this disastrous trade affect the development of Africa, and the relationship between Africans and Europeans?

It is hard for us to imagine the isolation of many of the African inland communities before the coming of the European – an isolation which increased their vulnerability to unscrupulous traders. Pope-Hennessey, a modern historian of Africa, describes a first meeting between the two cultures. "In the seventeenth century . . . even influential Africans who had never seen a white man supposed them to be a species of sea-monster, since they had heard that they came from over the horizon, where no land was, in large ships . . . *Mysterious Europeans*

"When the Danes were rebuilding Christiansborg . . . the Akyem King, Firempong, was made protector of the new fort for thirty-two dollars a month. Firempong had never yet seen a white man and, according to the Gold Coast missionary Rheindorf [an African scholar who published his *History of the Gold Coast and Ashanti* in 1895] he accepted the current hearsay that 'the Europeans were a kind of sea-creature.' Since he wanted to confirm this belief, he asked for a specimen to be sent to his town of Da. A Danish book-keeper, Nicholas Kamp, was despatched and found a formal reception awaiting him. But when he took off his hat and bowed, King Firempong, thinking he was a wild animal about to spring, fell flat on his face and yelled for the assistance of his wives. When the interpreter had explained that Kamp's queue [plait of hair] was not a tail growing from his neck, Firempong, still dissatisfied, demanded that Kamp strip naked. This the Danish book-keeper refused to do in public. After a meal watched by all the King's wives – one of whom remarked, 'He eats like a man, really he is a human being' – Kamp removed his clothes in private before the King. This convinced King Firempong: 'Ah, you really are a human being, but only too white, like a devil.' (45)" *King Firempong*

The arrival of the white men was a profound shock to African

37

Overleaf Conditions on the slave ships were appalling; many of the slaves died from disease or starvation

society. For the African, white was the colour of evil and of devils; Africans sold into slavery were convinced that they were about to be eaten by their white captors. But, most importantly, the arrival of the Europeans, with their increasing demand for slaves, disrupted communities which had been secure and peaceful.

King Affonso   As early as 1526 Affonso, the King of the Congo and a baptized Christian, complained to the Portuguese king about the activities of the Europeans. "Your Kingdom should know," he wrote,"how our Kingdom is being lost in so many ways that it is convenient to provide for the necessary remedy, since this is caused by the excessive freedom given by your factors [agents] and officials to the men and merchants who are allowed to come to this Kingdom to set shops with goods and many things which have been prohibited by us, and which they spread throughout our Kingdoms and domains in such an abundance that many of our vassals, whom we had in obedience, do not comply because they have the things in greater abundance than we ourselves (46)."

Greed for slaves   Already the greed for slaves was shattering the peace of Affonso's kingdom. "Merchants," he continued, "are taking every day our natives, sons of the land and the sons of our noblemen and vassals and our relatives. The thieves . . . grab them and get them to be sold; and so great, Sir, is the corruption and licentiousness that our country is being completely depopulated, and Your Highness should not agree with this nor accept it as in your service (47)."

Slave wars   Not only did wars among the African states supply Europeans with more slaves, the demand for slaves actually provoked wars. Olaudah Equiano, another freed slave, described wars which had occurred during his childhood in Africa: "From what I can recollect of these battles, they appear to have been irruptions of one little state or district on the other to obtain prisoners or booty. Perhaps they were incited to this by those traders who brought the European goods I mentioned amongst us. Such a mode of obtaining slaves in Africa is common (48)."

Moorish slave raiders   Of course there had been wars before the slave trade, but the increased value of the prisoners of war caused new conflicts, which were often encouraged by the Europeans. In 1789 C. B. Wadström, a Swedish traveller who had visited Africa, commented that "the Moors, who inhabit the countries on the north of the River Senegal, are particularly infamous for their predatory wars. They cross the river, and attacking the negroes, bring many of them off. There are not a few who subsist by means of these unprovoked excursions.

"The French, to encourage them in it, make annual presents to the Moorish kings. These are given them under certain conditions, first, that their subjects shall not carry any of their gum to the English at Portendic; and, secondly, that they shall be ready on all occasions, to furnish slaves. To enable them to fulfil this last article, they never fail to supply them with ammunition, guns, and other instruments of War (49)."

French encourage-ment

The introduction of fire-arms made wars between Africans far more destructive. In the mid-eighteenth century, Birmingham gunsmiths were said to be exporting 100,000 muskets to Africa each year.

Guns

William Bosman tried to justify the trade: "The chief [of the coastal Africans' military arms] are muskets or carabins, in the management of which they are wonderful dextrous.

"Perhaps," he continued, "you wonder how the negroes come to be furnished with fire-arms, but you will have no reason when you know we sell them incredible quantities, thereby obliging them with a knife to cut our own throats. But we are forced to it for if we would not, they might be sufficiently stored with that commodity by the English, Danes, and Brandenburghers (50)."

Arms trade

The whole development of West Africa was distorted by the European presence. Old kingdoms like Benin were swept away, and replaced by aggressive states such as Oyo and Dahomey. According to a contemporary account, when the Oyo went to war, "the general spreads the hide of a buffalo before the door of his tent, and pitches a spear in the ground, on each side of it. Between this the soldiers march, until the multitude, which pass over the hide, have worn a hole through it; as soon as this happens, he presumes that his forces are numerous enough to take the field (51)."

New kingdoms

Apart from introducing greater aggression into Africa, the

African slave traders

slave trade and its attendant evils corrupted African life in more subtle ways: "I must own," wrote Ottobah Cuguano, " . . . that I was first kidnapped and betrayed by my own complexion, who were the first cause of my exile and slavery. But if there were no buyers there would be no sellers. So far as I can remember, some of the Africans in my country kept slaves, which they take in war, or for debt. But those which they keep are well, and good care taken of them, and treated well . . . (52)"

Africans certainly played an important part in running the slave trade. Indeed, their co-operation was essential if the trade was to continue. The coastal forts, for instance, depended largely upon African labour. Without Africans as "blacksmiths, fishermen, canoe and house carpenters, salt boilers, potters, mat-makers, husbandmen, porters, watermen or paddlers and soldiers the forts could not have remained in existence. . . (53)"

Demoralized Europeans It was inevitable that many Africans cashed in on the corrupt business of buying and selling their fellow men. The activity had an equally demoralizing effect upon the European residents. "I observe most of our factors [agents]," wrote an English trader, "to have dwindled much from the genteel air they brought; wear no cane or snuff-box, idle in men of business, have lank bodies, a pale visage, their pockets sewn up or of no use, and their tongues tied. One cause of their slenderness indeed is a scarcity of provision; little beside plantain, small fish, Indian corn and a great deal of canky [alcoholic drink], to be bought at market (54)."

Indeed, it seemed that the slave trade tainted and destroyed everything it touched.

Anti-slavery campaign The campaign against the slave trade had been gradually growing since the late eighteenth century. At last, in 1807, the work of men such as Granville Sharp, William Wilberforce and Thomas Clarkson, was successful: the carrying of slaves in British ships was forbidden.

But the damage had been done. The terrible and lasting effect of the trade upon Africa was to affect the future growth of the continent. J. Hatch, in his recent history of Africa, sums up the

Opposite William Wilberforce, the English M.P., who led the campaign to abolish the slave trade in British overseas colonies

WILLIAM WILBERFORCE, M.P. THE FRIEND OF AFRICA.

I HAVE HEARD THEIR CRY

SLAVE TRADE ABOLISHED *Exod.III — 7.*

1807.

43

destructive impact of these centuries of exploitation: "Slave raiding and slave warfare destroyed political progress and created such uncertain conditions as to make any constructive future planning impossible. Life was for the moment; society itself had no stability or continuity. The inducements of the slave trade played a large part in the rise of Benin, Dahomey and Ashanti and in the growth of Oyo. Yet the obsession with acquiring wealth and power from the slave trade and the wars which fostered it, played an equally large part in their decline."

Increased aggression

He points out that: "Inter-state wars and civil wars, all for the promotion of slavery, inevitably undermined the structure of those states which had been built on these very activities. Provincial rulers revolted against the centre in order to secure a greater share in the trade. One state invaded another for the same purpose. Recruiting, training and paying armies took the place of developing the peaceful pursuits of social life. Economic organization was subordinated to the voracious, obsessive demands of securing the slave commodity in order to purchase more and yet more goods from European merchants. The development of those arts and techniques known in pre-slave trading days was almost entirely neglected (55)."

Coming change

But, even as the efforts of the anti-slavery campaigners were bringing the trade to an end, inventions and developments were being made in Europe that would fundamentally alter her relationship with Africa. Just as the earlier incursions of the Europeans on the east African coast had destroyed the balance of trade around the Indian Ocean, so the industrial revolution would shatter even more effectively the balance between the two continents.

3 Europe Discovers Africa

AT THE BEGINNING of the nineteenth century the interior of Africa was still a region of mystery to the white man. European traders kept to the extreme edge of the continent, living and dying in their coastal forts. They depended upon Africans and Arabs to keep them supplied with merchandise from the interior. Few Europeans, apart from the Portuguese in East Africa, had ventured far inland. Although the slave trade had profoundly affected the course of African history, the Europeans had neither the means nor the inclination to extend their interests beyond the coast.

Unknown continent

The industrial revolution of the nineteenth century made possible a fundamental change in this relationship between Africa and Europe. Europeans, with a new confidence in the superiority of their culture, opened up the continent through exploration. Then, using their superior technology, they conquered it and divided it among themselves.

New technology

The great period of African exploration started with Robert Bruce's journey to Ethiopia in 1769, and ended with the European partition of Africa in the 1880s. The interior of Africa was an appallingly inhospitable region for the white man, and the explorers faced terrifying obstacles in their efforts to penetrate it. Much of the continent was infected by the tsetse fly, which attacks and usually kills animals such as horses and mules. So human bearers had to be used to carry the burdens of an expedition.

Exploring Africa

"There are no such things," wrote Mrs. Melville, the wife of a British official on the coast, "as carts, waggons, or even

45

Overleaf Nineteenth-century explorers in Africa did not let the difficult terrain hinder their travels

hand-barrows in the place . . . Everything that one person is able to carry is borne upon the head . . . Unwieldy articles, such as casks, are slung upon poles of bamboo, which then are rested on the shoulders of several persons, while very large pieces of furniture are carried simply on the heads or shoulders of as many as are required to bear the weight (56)."

Palanquins   The lack of roads meant that Europeans were usually carried in a palanquin on the shoulders of the bearers. "There are two kinds," observed a contemporary traveller "One is the ordinary hammock, in which the occupant travels lying down, and the other is known as a sitting hammock. The latter is by far the more comfortable, and it certainly is not so hot; it has also the advantage of allowing the occupant to see where he is going. The angle of the sitting hammock can be changed by means of a foot rest, and this is a great relief to your tired body on a long day's journey . . .(57)"

Diseases   European explorers were afflicted by a variety of tropical diseases against which they had little resistance. "It is astonishing," a European nurse remarked, "how quickly that African fever prostrates a man, and with what equal rapidity he recovers – or dies – as the case may be. This is perhaps true only of its first attacks. Later on, when a man is saturated with malaria, he seems unable to shake off the fever. The recurrences are slight, but persistent, and it is then that complications arise and health is completely undermined (58)."

Lady Baker   Many explorers fell victim to disease; but perhaps the most tragic case was that of Lady Baker, who accompanied her husband on several of his expeditions. "For seven nights, I had not slept," wrote Baker after the ordeal, "and although as weak as a reed, I had marched by the side of her litter. Nature could resist no longer. We reached a village one evening; she had been in violent convulsions successively – it was all but over. I laid her down on her litter within a hut; covered her with a Scotch plaid; and I fell upon my mat insensible, worn out with sorrow and fatigue. My men put a new handle to the pickaxe that evening, and sought for a dry spot to dig her grave (59)."

Native   Quite unable to treat these unaccustomed diseases, Europeans
48   *remedies*   were often forced to try native cures, which sometimes seemed

Opposite Livingstone, like most Europeans in Africa, suffered from tropical diseases. Even travelling in a litter was a nightmare when wracked by fever

The animals of Africa were another danger faced by explorers. Living-stone was lucky – he escaped with only a broken arm

worse than the disease itself. Richard Lander tried one on his dying master, Hugh Clapperton: "On the 9th," he wrote in his report of the expedition, "Maddie [a servant], brought him about twelve ounces of green bark, from the butter-tree . . . , and assured us that it would produce the most beneficial effects. Notwithstanding all my remonstrances, a decoction of it was ordered to be prepared immediately, the too-confiding invalid remarking that no one would injure him. Accordingly, Maddie himself boiled two basins full, the whole of which stuff was swallowed in less than an hour (60)."

Another danger facing the explorers was attack by wild animals. A lion very nearly brought David Livingstone's work in Africa to a premature end. Livingstone thought that he had shot and killed the beast, but he was in for a nasty shock: "When in the act of ramming down the bullets I heard a shout. Starting, and looking half round, I saw the lion just in the act of springing upon me. I was upon a little height; he caught my shoulder as he sprang, and we both came to the ground below together. Growling horribly close to my ear, he shook me as a terrier dog does a rat. The shock produced a stupor similar to that which seems to be felt by a mouse after the first shake of a cat. . .

"Turning round to relieve myself of the weight, as he had one paw on the back of my head, I saw his eyes directed to Mebalwe, who was trying to shoot him at a distance of ten or fifteen yards . . . the lion immediately left me, and, attacking Mebalwe, bit his thigh.

"Another man . . . attempted to spear the lion while he was biting Mebalwe. He left Mebalwe and caught this man by the shoulder, but at that moment the bullets he had received took effect, and he fell down dead. The whole was the work of a few moments, and must have been his paroxysm of dying rage. . . Besides crunching the bone into splinters, he left eleven teeth wounds in the upper part of my arm (61)."

African chiefs were also likely to cause difficulties. It was essential to obtain their co-operation. According to Sir Richard Burton who travelled extensively in Africa, ". . . the etiquette is to send a messenger on to announce your coming, and to ask permission to draw nearer the august Black. Your name, height, and weight, and 'how many horses your father's got,' etc., should be stated, or particulars quite as ridiculous. The answer may be no and may be yes. If yes, you may approach entirely as a dependent before his lord, though he is jolly enough on a nearer acquaintance. You ask permission to hunt, and he gives it sometimes after several days' delay, and then you go in the direction he pleases, and his people see that you go in no other (62)."

Another English explorer, John Speke, had a similar experience. In his journal he described the uncooperative nature of

Dangerous animals

African chiefs

Chief Mtesa

Overleaf The reaction of the local people to European travellers was often unpredictable and sometimes fatal

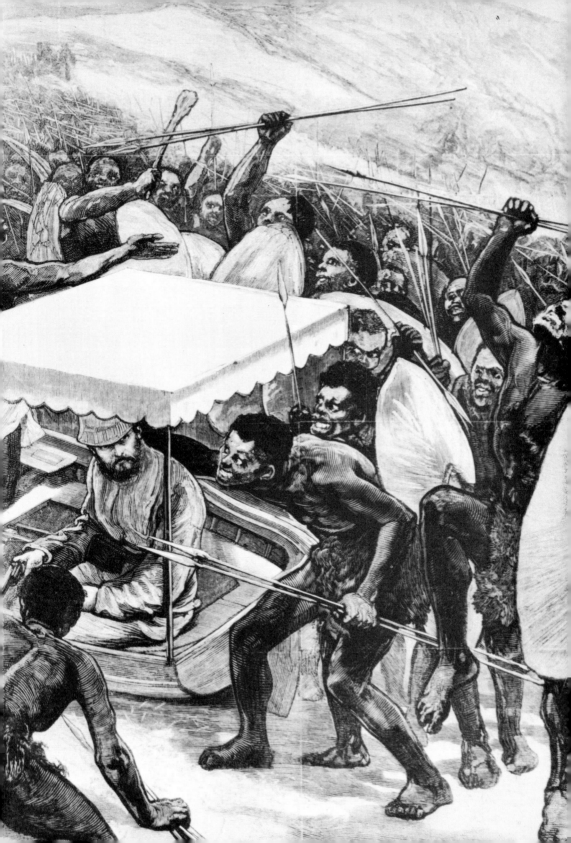

Mtesa, King of Buganda: "There were no guinea-fowls to be found here, nor a fowl in any of the huts, so I requested Rozaro to hurry off to Mtesa, and ask him to send me something to eat. He simply laughed at my request, and said I did not know what I was doing. It would be as much as my life was worth to go one yard in advance of this until the king's leave was obtained. I said, rather than be starved to death in this ignominious manner, I would return to Karague; to which he replied, laughing, 'Whose leave have you got to do that? Do you suppose you can do as you like in this country?' (63)"

King Kamrasi In 1864, Sir Samuel Baker discovered that the African king, Kamrasi, would allow him to continue his journey, but at a price: " 'I will send you to the lake and Shooa, as I have promised, but you must leave your wife behind with me,' said the King." Baker levelled his revolver at him saying "in undisguised contempt," that if the trigger were pulled not all his guards could save him, "and that if he dared to repeat the insult I would shoot him on the spot.

"At the same time I told him that in my country such insolence would entail bloodshed, and that I looked on him as an ignorant ox who knew no better, and that this excuse could alone save him. My wife, naturally indignant, had arisen from her seat, and made him a little speech in Arabic (not a word of which he understood) with a countenance almost as amiable as the head of Medusa (64)."

Excitement of In the face of such dangers and hardships, what drove Euro-
exploration pean travellers to continue exploring the continent? There is no doubt that Christian zeal to convert the Africans was a strong stimulus: "Now that I am on the point of starting on another trip into Africa," David Livingstone wrote in his diary, "I feel quite exhilarated. When one travels with the specific object in view of ameliorating the condition of the natives every act becomes ennobled . . . the sweat of one's brow is no longer a curse when one works for God (65)."

Sir Samuel Although excitement and the desire for adventure spurred
Baker many explorers, the real prize was the joy and exhilaration of being the first white man to set foot in unknown places. Sir Samuel Baker described his feelings as he approached Lake

All Europeans, whether explorers, traders, missionaries or settlers, were
likely to meet hostility from the natives

Albert: "That night I hardly slept. For years I had striven to reach the 'sources of the Nile.' In my nightly dreams during the arduous voyage I had always failed, but after so much hard work and perseverance the cup was at my very lips...

"I had hoped, and prayed, and striven through all kinds of difficulties, in sickness, starvation, and fatigue to reach that hidden source; and when it had appeared impossible we had both determined to die upon the road rather than return defeated. Was it possible that it was so near, and that to-morrow we could say, 'the work is accomplished?'

The goal   "The sun had not risen when I was spurring my ox after the guide, who, having been promised a double handful of beads on arrival at the lake, had caught the enthusiasm of the moment. The day broke beautifully clear, and having crossed a deep valley between the hills, we toiled up the opposite slope. I hurried to the summit. The glory of our prize burst suddenly upon me! There, like a sea of quick-silver, lay far beneath the grand expanse of water – a boundless sea horizon on the south and south-west glittering in the noon-day sun...

"It is impossible to describe the triumph of that moment; here was the reward for all our labour – for the years of tenacity with which we had toiled through Africa. England had won the sources of the Nile! (66)"

The Blue Nile   James Bruce expressed a similar sense of triumph when he stood at the source of the Blue Nile: "It is easier to guess than to describe the situation of my mind at that moment – standing in that spot which had baffled the genius, industry and inquiry of both ancients and moderns, for the course of near three thousand years. Kings had attempted this discovery at the head of armies and each expedition was distinguished from the last, only by the difference of the numbers which had perished, and agreed alone in the disappointment which had uniformly and without exception, followed them all.

Triumph   "Fame, riches and honour, had been held out for a series of ages to every individual of those myriads these princes commanded, without having produced one man capable of gratifying the curiosity of his sovereign, or wiping off this strain upon the enterprise and abilities of mankind, or adding this desideratum

Travel by river was no safer or easier than going overland

for the encouragement of geography. Though a mere private Briton, I triumphed here, in my own mind, over kings and their armies (67)."

This was the reward which drove men to surmount the dangers of disease, hardship and privation. Little more than a century after Bruce reached Ethiopia in 1769, European explorers had solved almost all the great geographical problems of the continent: white men had stood at the sources of the White and Blue Niles; the Niger and Congo rivers had been navigated; scarcely a corner of the continent had not felt the confident footsteps of Europeans.

The nineteenth-century explorers were extremely courageous men, and the accounts of their adventures and excitements are fascinating documents of human endeavour. But they also reveal

Africa explored

57

Overleaf Heavy, formal clothing was the fashion for Europeans in Africa. They thought it helped to show their superiority to the natives

the growth of a new relationship between the African and the European. Unlike the European traders of the previous centuries, these men were filled with complete confidence in the superiority of their race and culture.

Ignorance about Africa Explorers like Sir Samuel Baker were totally ignorant of the African past. "The natives of tropical countries do not progress," he wrote confidently, "enervated by intense heat, they incline rather to repose and amusement than to labour. Free from the rigours of winters, and the excitement of changes in the seasons, the native character assumes the monotony of their country's temperature. They have no natural difficulties to contend with – no struggle with adverse storms and icy winds and frost-bound soil; but an everlasting summer, and fertile ground producing with little tillage, excite no enterprise; and the human mind, unexercised by difficulties, sinks into languor and decay (68)."

Servants Baker, like most of the explorers, assumed that the natural relationship between African and European was that of master and servant. An English missionary's account of a typical camp shows this new relationship: "The first thing on arriving in camp is, for us, who have carried nothing heavier than an umbrella and a monstrous hat, to rest. For the men, who have carried a load of fifty to sixty pounds (sometimes more), generally on their heads, to fetch firewood and water . . .

"The contrast will have struck you already," he adds. "The people, to whom we have come to preach, lie on the ground or in a reed or grass hut, eat rice and a bit of dried fish . . . carry a load under a burning sun for ten or twelve miles which I should be sorry to carry for a mile in England, walk barefoot on the scorching ground, while we live in grand houses or tents (palaces to these people), sleep on beds as comfortable as any at home, eat chickens (carried in a box alive), preserved meat, green peas (preserved), tea, cocoa, biscuits, bread, butter, jam (69)."

European superiority The European had come to believe that he was a member of a superior species; it was his duty to assert and maintain that superiority at all times. So dignity was essential; heavy European clothes were worn in the heat of the tropical sun; hundreds of miles from civilization meals were prepared and eaten in a style more suited to a London dinner-party; wooden chairs were

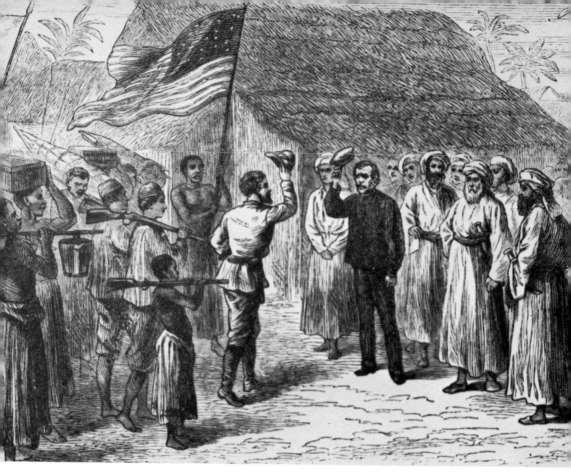

The historic moment when Stanley greeted Livingstone at Ujiji

carried into remote regions so that the European would not lose his dignity by sitting on the ground.

No unseemly display was allowed to mar the famous meeting between Stanley and Livingstone. "What would I not have given," wrote Stanley later, "for a bit of friendly wilderness, where, unseen, I might vent my joy in some mad freak, such as . . . turning a somersault, or slashing at trees, in order to allay those exciting feelings that were well-nigh uncontrollable. My heart beats fast, but I must not let my face betray my emotions, lest it shall detract from the dignity of a white man appearing under such extraordinary circumstances.

"So I did that which I thought was most dignified. I pushed back the crowds, and, passing from the rear, walked down a

Stanley meets Livingstone

living avenue of people, until I came in front of the semicircle of Arabs, in the front of which stood the white man with the grey beard. As I advanced slowly towards him I noticed he was pale, looked wearied, had a grey beard, wore a bluish cap with a faded gold band round it, had on a red-sleeved waistcoat, and a pair of grey tweed trousers. I would have run to him, only I was a coward in the presence of such mob – would have embraced him, only, he being an Englishman, I did not know how he would receive me; so I did what cowardice and false pride suggested was the best thing – walked deliberately to him, took off my hat, and said:

"'Dr. Livingstone, I presume?'

"'Yes,' said he, with a kind smile, lifting his cap slightly.

"I replace my hat on my head, and he puts on his cap, and we both grasp hands, and I then say aloud:

"'I thank God, Doctor, I have been permitted to see you.'

"He answered, 'I feel thankful that I am here to welcome you.' (70)"

Punishments If African servants and bearers were disobedient, European explorers did not hesitate to use violence. It was essential to demonstrate the superiority of the European. As Sir Frederick Lugard explained: "The whole influence of the European in Africa is gained by this assertion of a superiority which commands the respect and excites the emulation of the savage. To forego this vantage-ground is to lose influence for good... [The European] must at all times assert himself, and repel an insolent familiarity, which is a thing entirely apart from friendship born of respect and affection. His dwelling-house should be as superior to those of the natives as he is himself superior to them (71)."

An uncomfortable cuff Lugard had his own ways of expressing the inherent superiority of the European; he describes what happened when an African insulted him: "Not liking to strike a native with my fist, I gave him a heavy box on the ear. He seemed inclined to show fight, for he was a strong-built man, but received another similar cuff, which effectually silenced him, but unfortunately broke a bone in my hand, spraining also my thumb and wrist against his cast-iron head. This caused me very great pain subsequently, and

my hand became perfectly useless, nor did I regain the full use
of it for a month or more (72)."

From these and other contemporary accounts, it is clear that *European*
the relationship between Africa and Europe had radically *ignorance*
altered by the mid-nineteenth century. The Victorian explorers
knew nothing of the splendours of the African past. Memories
of Ghana, Mali and Songhai, of the cities of Zenj and the
inland states of medieval Rhodesia and Mozambique had
vanished. Baker confidently told a British audience that:
"Central Africa . . . is without a history. In that savage country
. . . we find no vestiges of the past – no ancient architecture, neither
sculpture, nor even one chiselled stone to prove that the Negro
savage of this day is inferior to a remote ancestor. . . We must
therefore conclude that the races of man which now inhabit
[this region] are unchanged from the prehistoric tribes who were
the original inhabitants (73)."

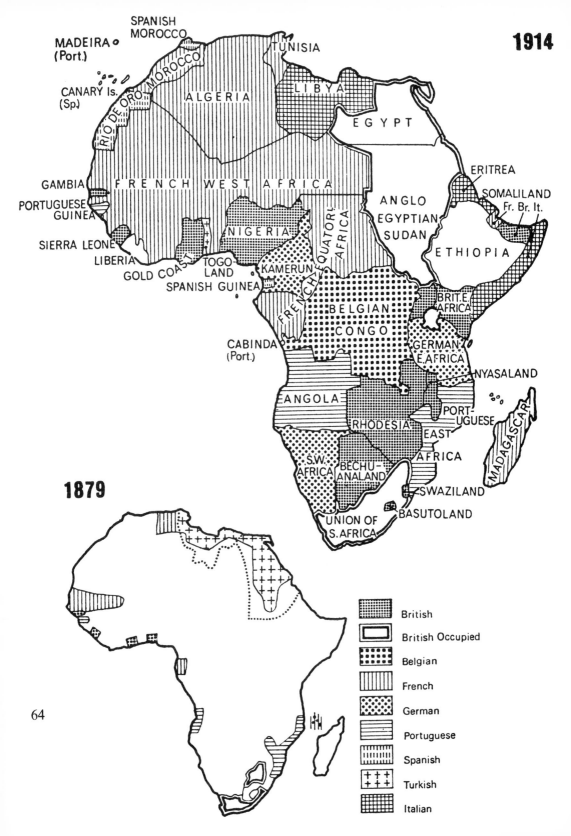

1914

MADEIRA (Port.)

SPANISH MOROCCO

TUNISIA

CANARY Is. (Sp.)

MOROCCO

RIO DE ORO

ALGERIA

LIBYA

EGYPT

ERITREA

GAMBIA

FRENCH WEST AFRICA

SOMALILAND Fr. Br. It.

PORTUGUESE GUINEA

ANGLO EGYPTIAN SUDAN

SIERRA LEONE

NIGERIA

FRENCH EQUATORIAL AFRICA

ETHIOPIA

LIBERIA

GOLD COAST

TOGO-LAND

KAMERUN

SPANISH GUINEA

BRIT. E. AFRICA

CABINDA (Port.)

BELGIAN CONGO

GERMAN E.AFRICA

NYASALAND

ANGOLA

PORT-UGUESE EAST AFRICA

MADAGASCAR

RHODESIA

S.W. AFRICA

BECHU-ANALAND

SWAZILAND

BASUTOLAND

UNION OF S.AFRICA

1879

64

	British
	British Occupied
	Belgian
	French
	German
	Portuguese
	Spanish
+++	Turkish
	Italian

4 Europe Conquers Africa

AFRICA HAD BEEN brought to Europe's attention by the activities of the explorers. But, until the last quarter of the nineteenth century, the idea that European states should use their new technical superiority to conquer and rule African territory was generally viewed with hostility.

However, small areas of the continent were already under white control: as early as 1652, Dutch immigrants had begun to build white settlements in the South; in the eighteen-thirties and forties, French armies had conquered part of North Africa; the British and the Portuguese controlled small enclaves of territory near the coast. *Early European colonies*

But even as late as 1866, Benjamin Disraeli, who later did so much to build up the British Empire, wrote to Lord Derby saying: "Power and influence we should exercise in Asia; consequently in Eastern Europe, consequently also in Western Europe; but what is the use of these colonial deadweights which we do not govern? . . . Leave the Canadians to defend themselves; recall the African squadron; give up the settlements on the west coast of Africa; and we shall make a saving which will, at the same time, enable us to build ships and have a good Budget (74)." *Disraeli*

Yet within fifty years of Disraeli's remarks virtually the whole of the African continent, apart from the ancient Kingdom of Ethiopia, was in European hands, and statesmen were convinced that national survival depended upon an overseas empire. What caused this sudden enthusiasm for conquest?

Part of the answer lies in the changes which had occurred in Europe since the end of the eighteenth century. "Steam and *European technology* 65

Opposite Africa before and after European countries scrambled for colonies in the "Dark Continent"

C

electricity have annihilated distance," wrote King Leopold of Belgium. "All the non-appropriated lands on the surface of the globe can become the field of our operations and success (75)." The Englishman, Sir John Seeley, argued that "science has given the political organism a new circulation, which is steam, and a new nervous system, which is electricity. These new conditions make it necessary to reconsider the whole colonial problem (76)."

African helplessness

Due to a fortunate coincidence of climate, resources and political development, Europe experienced her industrial revolution before Africa. As a result, Africa was helpless before the steamships, dynamite, and machine guns of European states, who were able to partition the continent at their leisure.

By the 1880s, the whole of Europe had become – or was becoming – industrialized. Competition for markets, raw materials and fields of investment made expansion necessary. Yet it was impossible for any state to expand in Europe itself without provoking a war.

Need for colonies

As early as 1870, John Ruskin suggested an answer to the dilemma: "This is what [England] must do, or perish," he proclaimed, "she must found colonies as fast and as far as she is able, . . . teaching her colonists that their chief virtue is fidelity to their country, and that their first aim is to advance the power of England by land and sea (77)."

Economic crisis

The feeling that European economies must expand at all costs was the constant theme of the French statesman, Jules Ferry: "Is it not clear," he asked the National Assembly, "that the great states of modern Europe, the moment their industrial power is founded, are confronted with an immense and difficult problem, which is the basis of industrial life, the very condition of existence – the question of markets? . . . European consumption is saturated: it is necessary to raise new masses of consumers in other parts of the globe, else we shall put modern society into bankruptcy and prepare for the dawn of the twentieth century a cataclysmic social liquidation of which one cannot calculate the consequences (78)."

The solution of these problems was as clear to Ferry, as it was to other French supporters of colonialism: "Colonization, is for France a question of life and death: either France will

Sheffield – a booming city of the Industrial Revolution. The need for
markets and raw materials led the industrialized European countries to
partition the African continent

become a great African power, or in a century or two she will be not more than a secondary European power; she will count for about as much in the world as Greece and Roumania in Europe (79)."

Joseph Chamberlain

In England, Joseph Chamberlain was perhaps the greatest exponent of a colonial policy. He was convinced that Britain could not exist without overseas possessions: "Is there any man in his senses," he asked in 1888, "who believes that the crowded population of these islands could exist for a single day if we were to cut adrift from us the great dependencies which now look to us for protection and assistance, and which are the natural markets for our trade? . . . If tomorrow it were possible, . . . to reduce . . . the British Empire to the dimensions of the United Kingdom, half at least of our population would be starved (80)."

Evolutionary ideas

But economic reasons were not the only ones for expansion. Many people, influenced by the ideas of Charles Darwin, came to believe that nations must struggle for survival in order to assert their superiority. "In every particular state of the world," wrote the philosopher, Walter Bagehot, "those nations which are the strongest tend to prevail over the others; and in certain marked peculiarities the strongest tend to be the best. The strongest nation has always been conquering the weaker. The majority of groups which win and conquer are better than the majority of those which fail and perish, and thus the first world grew better and was improved (81)."

Prelude to war

Some people drew disturbing conclusions from these ideas: "The foreign policies of the nations," wrote an anonymous contributor to the *Saturday Review*, "so far as they are not the mere expressions of the individual ambitions of rulers, or the jog-trot opportunism of diplomatists, are anticipation of, and provision for, struggles for existence between incipient species. . . The facts are patent. Feeble races are being wiped off the earth and the few great, incipient species arm themselves against each other (82)."

The scramble for colonies

With ideas like these in vogue it was inevitable that covetous eyes would be turned towards the vast, underpopulated, and defenceless continent of Africa.

In 1881 the French proclaimed a protectorate over Tunis. In

1882 the British, seeking to protect the Suez Canal which had been opened in 1869, established control over Egypt. In 1885 the King of Belgium annexed the Congo. Even the German Chancellor Bismarck, who opposed colonialism, was forced to admit that "a great nation like Germany could not, in the end, dispense with colonies (83)."

Once partition started, the process gathered momentum: each country grabbing as much as it could to prevent others grabbing more. No country could afford to be left behind.

"It is said that our Empire is already large enough," Lord Rosebery told the Colonial Institute in 1893, "and does not need extension. That would be true enough if the world were elastic, but unfortunately it is not elastic . . .

Lord Rosebery

"We have to look forward," he went on, "to the future of the want in the future. We have to consider what countries must be developed either by ourselves or some other nation, and we have to remember that it is part of our responsibility and heritage to take care that the world, so far as it can be moulded by us, shall receive an English-speaking complexion, and not that of other nations. . .

"We have to look forward," he went on, "to the future of the race of which we are at present the trustees, and we should, in my opinion, grossly fail in the task that has been laid upon us did we shrink from responsibilities and decline to take our share in a partition of the world which we have not forced on, but which has been forced upon us (84)."

Surprisingly, the "scramble for Africa" did not lead to wars between European states. European powers usually settled any conflicting interests by negotiation or by great international conferences. Such a conference was held in Berlin in 1884, to settle the fate of West Africa. Needless to say, no African representative was present at the negotiations.

Avoiding wars

The nearest the powers came to war over Africa was the Fashoda incident of 1898. The British feared that a foreign power might gain control of the Upper Nile and interfere with the flow of Nile water, on which Egypt depended. "It is an uncomfortable thought," wrote Lord Milner in 1892, "that

Fashoda incident

69

Overleaf The ceremonial opening of the Suez Canal, 16th November, 1869

the regular supply of water by the great river, which is to Egypt not a question of convenience and prosperity but actually of life, must always be exposed to some risk, as long as the upper reaches of that river are not under Egyptian [i.e. English] control (85)."

However, the French saw no reason why the Nile valley should be an exclusively British preserve. So, in 1896, a small expedition under Captain Marchand was sent from French West Africa "to remove all pretext for the occupation of Egypt by the English and to put an end to the dream of our dear friends, who wish to unite Egypt with the Cape and their possessions in East Africa with those of the Royal Niger Company (86)."

Foreign Office reaction The reaction of the British Foreign Office to rumours of Marchand's expedition was icy. The British Foreign Secretary, Sir Edward Grey, told the House of Commons that he had "no reason to suppose that any French Expedition has instructions to enter, or the intention of entering, the Nile Valley.

"I cannot think," he said, "that these rumours deserve credence, because the advance of a French expedition under secret instructions right from the other side of Africa, into a territory over which our claims have been known for so long, would be not merely an inconsistent and unexpected act, but it must be perfectly well known to the French Government that it would be an unfriendly act, and would be so viewed by England (87)."

Confrontation When, in 1898, Marchand's small force confronted a British army under General Kitchener at Fashoda, the world held its breath, fearing a European war. But, after a tense period of confrontation, the French climbed down. Europe's African diplomacy returned to its usual greedy, but gentlemanly manner; and by 1898 there was little of Africa left to scramble for.

African resistance Any resistance by the Africans had little hope of success. The potent weapons of the industrial societies made them victims or spectators as the European states carved up their homelands. Usually, African resistance was received with contempt: "It seemed rather a pitiful thing," wrote a British officer about an expedition against the Matabele people, "the Great Imperial Army mounted outside those caves and a bunch of niggers and

Captain Marchand and his troops going to Fashoda

their women lying up terrified inside and we trampling and bivouacking in their little gardens outside. . ."

His account of the incident continues: "We traced the living quarters of the blacks, working in the ground overhead of their caves, which ran for a quarter of a mile underground. Our blacks dug a huge hole, we put down six cases of dynamite, laid the detonators and stood clear. There was a horrible bang and out shot the Matabele (88)."

Certain powerful tribes, like the Ashanti and the Zulu, put up a brave resistance, but stood no chance against modern weapons.

But there were a few exceptions. In 1896, for instance, the army of the Ethiopian Emperor Menelek wiped out a large Italian force at Adowa. In 1881, a great religious leader, the Mahdi, appeared in the Sudan. Proclaiming a Jihad, or Holy

The Mahdi

73

Home of a Boer farmer, 1881. It looks like a European cottage

War, against the corrupt Egyptian administration, the Mahdi's armies swept all before them. An Egyptian army of 10,000 under the British general, Hicks Pasha, was wiped out in 1883. In 1885 the Mahdi's armies took the city of Khartoum and killed General Gordon, one of the great heroes of Victorian Britain.

Battle of Omdurman   The British had to wait thirteen years, but they got their revenge for Gordon's death. In 1898, General Kitchener, with a force of twenty thousand, came face to face with the Mahdi's army of fifty thousand at Omdurman.

The young Winston Churchill was present and described the scene: "Suddenly the whole black line which seemed to be the Zeriba [a defence work of branches and thorns] began to move. It was made of men, not bushes. Behind it other immense masses and lines of men appeared over the crest; and while we watched amazed by the wonder of the sight, the whole face of the slope beneath become black with swarming savages. Four miles from end to end, and, as it seemed, in five great divisions, this mighty army advanced – swiftly. The whole side of the hill seemed to move. Behind the masses horsemen galloped continually; before them many patrols dotted the plain; above them waved hundreds of banners, and the sun, glinting on many thousand hostile spear-points, spread a sparkling cloud (89)."

Despite the terrifying appearance of the Mahdi's army, the spears of his warriors stood no chance against the Maxim guns and artillery of the British. "It was not a battle, it was an execution (83)," wrote Churchill. In a few hours, 11,000 of the Mahdi's followers lay heaped in the desert. The British losses were 500. "At half past eleven," Churchill recorded, "Sir H. Kitchener shut up his glasses, remarking that he thought the enemy had been given 'a good dusting' (90)." *Mahdi defeated*

During the creation of European empires in Africa, wars between the powers had been avoided, partly by diplomacy, partly by self-interest. But, on the eve of the twentieth century, the British were faced by a small, but unexpectedly determined, adversary. The two small Republics of the Transvaal and the Orange Free State dared to attempt what great powers had avoided: they challenged the relentless expansion of the British Empire. *Britain challenged*

The first Dutch settlers had arrived in Africa in 1652. During the next two centuries they founded independent farming communities around the Cape. These farmers, or Boers, had a fierce Protestant faith. Confident that they were God's elect, they believed, equally strongly, in their superiority over the native Africans, regarding them merely as "hewers of wood, and drawers of water." *The Boers*

David Livingstone found the Boer attitude to the Africans disturbing: "I have myself been an eyewitness of Boers coming to a village," he wrote, "and, according to their usual custom, demanding twenty or thirty women to weed their gardens, and have seen these women proceed to the scene of unrequited toil, carrying their own food on their heads, their children on their backs and instruments of labour on their shoulders. Nor have the Boers any wish to conceal the meanness of thus employing unpaid labour. On the contrary, every one . . . lauded his own *African servants*

75

Overleaf Cecil Rhodes, a prominent figure in the development of southern Africa, with a group of friends

humanity and justice in making such an equitable regulation. 'We make the people work for us, in consideration of allowing them to live in our country' (91)."

Boer republics set up

In 1834, the British, who had taken over from the Dutch in South Africa during the Napoleonic Wars, ended slavery throughout the British Empire. The Boer way of life depended on slavery; and after the Abolition Act many decided they could no longer tolerate British rule. So they left their homes, trekking many miles to set up their own republics of Transvaal and Orange Free State beyond the jurisdiction of the British Government. In 1881 the British tried to take over the two republics, but their army was defeated at Majuba Hill, and the Boers clung stubbornly to their independence.

Gold and diamonds

For the next twenty years, Britain and the republics maintained a strained truce. But then two discoveries were made which affected the whole future of southern Africa. In 1870, diamonds were found in the Orange Free State; and in 1886, gold was discovered by the ton at Witwatersrand in the Transvaal. Instantly the calm of the farming republics was shattered. Hordes of speculators flocked from every corner of the world to make their fortunes on the Rand.

Cecil Rhodes

The Englishman, Cecil John Rhodes, was one of the first. Rhodes arrived in Africa in 1870. By 1880 he had founded De Beers Mining Company and become a millionaire; by 1887 he was head of the British South Africa Company; by 1890 he was President of Cape Colony and the most powerful man in South Africa.

Rhodes had the worst characteristics of the late Victorian imperialists. Aggressively patriotic, he made no secret of his aim to extend the British Empire by any way possible. "I'll take their country from them (92)," was his unashamed threat to anyone opposing him. Rhodes was prepared to use his wealth and energy to paint the map red (the colour in which British colonies were marked) from the Cape to Cairo. He was confident of enthusiastic support: "The people have found that England is small, and her trade large, and they have also found out that other people are taking their share of the world, and enforcing hostile tariffs. The people of England are finding out that 'trade follows the flag' and they have all become Imperialists. They are not going to part with any territory. . . The English people intend to retain every inch of land they have got, and perhaps they intend to secure a few more inches (93)."

To men like Rhodes, it was intolerable that the gold and diamond mines of the Rand should be controlled by the stolid Boer farmers under their aged president, Paul Kruger. Thousands of Uitlanders (foreigners), had flocked into the Republics seeking their fortunes. But, as Rhodes frequently reminded the British Government, although the Boers taxed these people, they allowed them no political rights. Isolated incidents of brutality inflamed British public opinion and Rhodes urged the Government to intervene. Again he recognized the mood of the people, expressed by the poet Alfred Austin (94): *Uitlanders*

> *There are girls in the gold-reef city,*
> *There are mothers and children too!*
> *And they cry, "Hurry up! For pity!"*
> *So what can a brave man do?*

Rhodes had no doubts about what he should do; he sent a raiding party into Boer territory under the command of his doctor friend, Robert Starr Jameson. Unfortunately for Rhodes the Uitlanders failed to respond to his heavy-handed assistance. Jameson and his column were captured and imprisoned and Rhodes was disgraced and forced to resign his presidency. *The Jameson raid*

After the Jameson raid relations between Britain and the Boer Republics deteriorated. British public opinion was enraged by a telegram sent to President Kruger by the Kaiser of Germany: "I express to you," the Kaiser wrote, "my sincere congratulations that you and your people, without appealing to the help of friendly powers, have succeeded, by your own energetic action against the armed bands which invaded your country as disturbers of the peace, in restoring peace and in maintaining the independence of the country against attacks from without (95)." *Kaiser's telegram*

After the arrival of the new British High Commissioner to South Africa, Alfred Milner, it became clear that Britain was prepared to take her vendetta with the Boers to the point of war.

Defence worries Milner and his superior at the Colonial Office, Joseph Chamberlain, were convinced that Britain had vital commercial and strategic interests at stake. Many foreign observers realized this: "The maintenance of the Cape Colony," wrote one diplomat, "was perhaps the most vital interest of Great Britain because by the possession of it communication with India was assured, which otherwise might be cut off any day. Cape Colony was of even greater importance to England than Malta or Gibraltar (96)."

War In 1899, the crisis between the British and Boers worsened. Neither Milner nor President Kruger would give way. So, on 12th October, war was declared.

Most people in Britain believed that the war would be a short one. It seemed impossible that a few thousand ill-trained and badly armed farmers would be able to defy the might of the British army for long. But as the war progressed it soon became apparent that all was not well.

Britain's weak position "The war exposed," wrote a contemporary journalist, "the complete isolation of Britain in the world. The Turkish Sultan was encouraged to kill more Armenians; the German Emperor exhilarated; President Kruger edified before Providence. The Uitlanders were weakened and divided . . . (97)"

It was clear, too, that the Boers' lack of military training was offset by their knowledge of the country, good commanders and the hardiness of men used to frontier life. The Boer army was a formidable one: "As far as the eye could see," wrote a young Boer commando, "the plain was alive with horsemen, guns and cattle, all steadily going forward to the frontier. The scene was a stirring one, and I shall never forget riding to war with that great host (98)."

Boer successes Within a fortnight of the declaration of war, the British army, under General Redvers Buller, was driven back and besieged in three strategic towns, Kimberly, Ladysmith and Mafeking. In the second week of December – Black Week, as it was known in Britain – the Boers successively defeated Generals Gatacre, Methuen and Buller.

The mood in London swept from exultation to despair: "The

Opposite British troops charging a Boer stronghold during the Boer War, 1899–1902

news was published on a grey raw day. In London people bought up the early editions of the evening journals . . . There was neither noise nor gesture. The news was read, the journals were not flung down, but folded and kept. Few men desired speech with their neighbours. It was certain from them, whatever this war might bring, that national will never would give in (99)."

The arrival of fresh troops in South Africa did not stop the Boer advances; and the demands for General Buller's replacement grew. The *Times History* was scathing about his failure: "Just as in the crisis of the battle he had failed the men whom he had led, so now in the hour of trial, he was to fail the country which had entrusted the fortune of war into his hands (100)." Buller was replaced by General Roberts, and Kitchener, the hero of Omdurman and Fashoda, became his chief-of-staff.

General Buller

Roberts' arrival transformed British fortunes. Throughout the spring of 1900 the Boers were gradually defeated and driven back. In February, first Kimberly and then Ladysmith were relieved, and Roberts, or "Bobs" as he was nicknamed, became a national hero. Rudyard Kipling wrote a poem about him (101):

General Roberts

> *There's a little red-faced man,*
> *Which is Bobs,*
> *Rides the tallest 'orse 'e can,*
> *Our Bobs.*
> *If it bucks or kicks or rears,*
> *'E can sit for twenty years*
> *With a smile round both 'is ears,*
> *Can't yer, Bobs?*

The greatest triumph of the year was the relief of Mafeking on 17th May. The besieged garrison had become a symbol of British fortitude and determination, and when news of the relief reached England there were extraordinary scenes of jubilation: "White-haired old ladies were to be seen carrying a large Union Jack in each hand, and young women had colours pinned across from shoulder to shoulder. Sober-looking young men in spectacles stood at street corners blowing tin trumpets with all

Relief of Mafeking

The relief of Mafeking: the good news reaches Britain

their might . . . Well-dressed young women of usually proper demeanour traversed the road-ways, arm-in-arm, six abreast, carrying flags and occasionally bursting into song. . . In Fleet Street a gentleman, . . . evidently from the United States, having burdened himself with more star-spangled banners than he could attach to his hat, shoulders, coat and trousers, unfolded a large umbrella and fastened to it the remainder of his stock . . . and walked thus up the street with perfect composure in a great halo of colour (102)."

Victory celebrations   Some of these celebrations even reached the Prime Minister's austere residence at Hatfield, as his daughter, Lady Gwendoline Cecil, relates: "Several scores of the inhabitants of Hatfield dressed themselves up as soldiers, sailors, nurses, heaven knows what, arranged in symbolical groups with horses and cars and properties of all kinds, and marched through the Parish by night with torches, flags, and bands playing . . . with the mass of torches in front of the old house, and the shouting, cheering crowd it was really quite thrilling (103)."

On 11th September, 1900, President Kruger was forced to flee to Portuguese Africa, and on 25th October, the British annexed the defeated Transvaal Republic. To distant Londoners it seemed as if the war was over.

The war continues   In fact the war dragged on for another eighteen months. The Boer armies had been defeated, but not destroyed. Under the leadership of their Vice-President, Schalk Burger, and General Louis Botha, they continued to use their commandos – swiftly moving groups of light cavalry – to harass the British forces. Some British officers were outraged by this type of warfare: "The bandit forces of Boer and Colonial rebels," wrote one Englishman, "are scouring the country from every direction, robbing, looting and house-burning . . . the [entire] country is overrun by small bands of rebels who are absolutely reckless of their lives and equally indifferent to the ordinary requirements of civilized warfare (104)."

Ruthless reprisals   The British were forced to use ruthless counter-measures. They issued a proclamation exiling all commandos who would not surrender. "All commandants, field cornets and leaders of armed bands," it read: "being burghers of the late Republics, still engaged in resisting Her Majesty's Forces . . . shall, unless they surrender before 15th September next, be permanently banished from South Africa; the cost of the maintenance of the families of all burghers in the field who shall not have surrendered by 15th September shall be recoverable from such burghers, and shall be a charge upon their property, moveable and immoveable, in the two Colonies (105).''

The open veld (countryside) was divided into sections by barbed wire fences and fortified block-houses, and any farm suspected of harbouring commandos was destroyed. A British officer describes what this entailed: "Farm-burning goes merrily on, and our course through the country is marked as in prehistoric ages by pillars of smoke by day and fire by night. We usually burn from six to a dozen farms a day; these being about all that in this sparsely-inhabited country we encounter." *Burning of farms*

He goes on to say: "I do not gather that any special reason or cause is alleged or proved against the farms burnt. If Boers have used the farm; if the owner is on commando; if the line within a certain distance has been blown up; or even if there are Boers in the neighbourhood who persist in fighting – these are some of the reasons. Of course the people living in the farms have no say in these matters, and are quite powerless to interfere with the plans of the fighting Boers. Anyway . . . one reason or another generally covers pretty nearly every farm we come to, and so to save trouble we burn the lot without enquiry; unless indeed, which sometimes happens, some names are given in . . . of farms to be spared (106)."

Often, it seems, the farm burning was carried out indiscriminately: "I hear that out of five farms which Arthur Paget burned in a single day one belonged to his own interpreter, one to a man whose wife has been nursing our men and one to a man in Kitchener's Horse (107)."

However, the "concentration camps" set up by the British authorities were the most unpopular counter-measure. Thousands of Boer women and children were herded into the camps; they were not deliberately ill-treated, but poor sanitation, bad food, and disease, caused the deaths of many. *"Concentration camps"*

The Liberal Party leader, Sir Henry Campbell-Bannerman, *Campbell-Bannerman* 85 was one of the few British politicians with the courage to speak out against these practices. "Where are the elements for a settlement in . . . South Africa?" he asked the Government. "The whole country in the two belligerent States outside the mining towns is a howling wilderness. The farms are burned, the country is wasted. The flocks and the herds are either butchered or driven off; the mills are destroyed, furniture and implements of agriculture are smashed. These things are what I have termed methods of barbarism. I adhere to the phrase. I cannot improve upon it. If these are not the methods of barbarism what methods did barbarism employ? (108)"

Peace   Despite these efforts to crush the Boers, the war dragged on. But both sides were becoming weary of it. In 1902 peace was signed at Vereeniging. For the British, the war had been a shock to national self-esteem; the mood in 1902 was very different from the unthinking self-confidence evident at the outbreak of the war. Survival in the face of British strength had increased the Boers' confidence in the unique qualities of their race, and the superiority of their exclusive way of life.

5 The Colonial Era

White rule

AT THE BEGINNING of the twentieth century, Africa lay under European domination. The speed of the conquest, and the feebleness of African resistance, had convinced many that they had a duty, as well as a right, to rule.

"Every Englishman," wrote Bernard Shaw, "is born with a certain miraculous power that makes him master of the world. When he wants a thing he never tells himself that he wants it. He waits patiently till there comes into his head, no one knows how, the burning conviction that it is his moral and religious duty to conquer those who have the thing he wants. Then he becomes irresistible. Like the aristocrat, he does what pleases him and grabs what he wants. Like the shopkeeper, he pursues his purpose with the industry and steadfastness that come from strong religious conviction and deep sense of moral responsibility. He is never at a loss for an effective moral attitude.

"As the great champion of freedom and independence," Shaw continues sarcastically, "he conquers half the world and calls it Colonization. When he wants a new market for his adulterated Manchester goods, he sends a missionary to teach the gospel of peace. The natives kill the missionary; he flies to arms in defence of Christianity; fights for it, conquers for it; and takes the market as a reward of heaven (109)."

European politicians and administrators were convinced that colonial rule brought immense benefits to the conquered. "Whenever the Empire has extended its borders," proclaimed Lord Curzon, Viceroy of India, "there misery and oppression,

Benefits of imperialism

anarchy and destitution, superstition and bigotry, have tended to disappear, and have been replaced by peace, justice, prosperity, humanity, and freedom of thought, speech, and action . . .

"Imperialism is . . . animated by the supreme idea . . . the sense of sacrifice and the idea of duty. Empire can only be achieved with satisfaction or maintained with advantage provided it has a moral basis. To the people of the mother state it must be a discipline, an inspiration, and a faith (110)."

Moral responsibilities This feeling, that the European states had a moral duty to assist the backward continents, was widespread. The poet Rudyard Kipling urged Christian white men to shoulder their responsibilities (111):

Take up the White Man's burden
The savage wars of peace –
Fill full the mouth of Famine
And bid the sickness cease;
And when your goal is nearest
The end for others sought,
Watch Sloth and heathen Folly
Bring all your hope to nought . . .

African inferiority This moral justification of white rule rested on the belief that the African was a child-like being – a being at an earlier stage of evolution to the European. "In spite of all our humanitarian goodwill," wrote a Belgian visitor, after a brief trip to the Congo in 1896, "we have to acknowledge the irreducible difference of race between us; no Christian dreams, no well-intentioned efforts to project to them our own sentiments, our thoughts, our capacities, can change this. . . .

"Like monkeys," he continues patronizingly, "the blacks are good imitators – to a surprising degree. One sees here . . . masons, blacksmiths, mechanics who have become really skilful. . . It is this undeniable dexterity of theirs which has given birth to an illusion. . . on the part of those who cannot distinguish between an imitator and a creator. Here, in fact, is the unbridgeable gulf. The negro can collaborate with the white man as a subaltern, he can correctly carry out a concrete

European missionaries followed the explorers to Africa. Unfortunately, they probably did as much harm as good, because their ideas were so alien to the African way of life

Red Cross sisters at a pioneer camp in the African bush, 1891

individual piece of work. . .

"But will he ever feel stirring in himself the need to be free from social servitude? . . . Will he ever see invisible realities, the hidden links in society, the way things hold together – a necessity for men of our race? Will he not always be a disguised slave, indirectly a serf, in carrying out his partial and localized tasks under the domination of the white man?

"Perhaps," he concludes smugly, "this is why, instinctively, the white scorns the black, and the black shows a natural submission, a childish humility, a reverential and timid awe before the white man (112)."

Untrustworthy Africans A similar view was expressed by the English writer, J. M. Ballantyne: "To treat him [the African] kindly, justly, considerately, lovingly, to try to do him every possible good, and chiefly, to bring his soul in contact with the Saviour, is our simple duty, but to trust him is no part of our duty. It is worse than folly because it defeats our philanthropic views and prolongs his debasement. Who would trust a thief, or a liar, or a murderer? The whole Kafir nation, root and branch, is a huge thief, an inveterate liar, and a wholesale murderer (113)."

If one could believe the missionaries and administrators, Europeans only conquered Africa to save its soul. A more realistic reason for European rule was given by Lord Lugard: "Let it be admitted at the outset," he wrote, "that European brains, capital, and energy have not been, and never will be, expended in developing the resources of Africa from motives of pure philanthropy; that Europe is in Africa for the mutual benefit of her own industrial classes, and of the native races in their progress to a higher plane; that the benefit can be made reciprocal, and that it is the aim and desire of civilized administration to fulfill this dual mandate (114)."

Reasons for imperialism

The great French administrator, Marshall Lyautey, was equally frank. He intended "to keep Morocco for France until the end, not only as a possession or as a conquered prize, but as a reserve of resources of all kinds for the mother-country (115)."

In 1933, the German politician Franz Von Papen wrote a treatise demanding the return of the German colonies. In it he explained why colonies were necessary to European states:

Importance of colonies

"Colonies, I repeat, are an economic necessity for Germany for four reasons:

"To feed her own people.

"To take care of her surplus population.

"To meet her foreign credit engagements, especially her private loans.

"To afford her an opportunity of spreading culture and civilization (116)."

Generally, as the great British administrator, Sir Harry Johnston, explained, European states had conquered Africa in order to exploit its wealth: "It somehow shocks the sense of fairness of hard-headed White or Yellow people," he wrote in 1920, "that semi-savages should be driving ill-bred sheep, scraggy cattle or ponies hardly fit for polo over plains and mountains that are little else than great treasure-vaults of valuable minerals and chemicals; or that they should roam with

Exploitation of Africa

their blow-pipes and bows and arrows through forests of inestimable value for their timber, drugs, dyes, latices, gums, oil-seeds, nuts or fruits; be turning this waiting wealth to no use, not allowing it to circulate in the world's markets (117)."

Peace in Africa   But did Africa benefit from European rule? At first sight the answer seems obvious: Europe brought to Africa the benefits of an advanced technology which transformed the face of the continent, and European rule stopped the inter-tribal wars which followed the break up of the medieval African states and the growth of the slave trade.

Sir Frederick Lugard   Sir Frederick Lugard had no doubts about the blessings of British rule: "By railroads and roads, by reclamation of swamps and irrigation of deserts, and by a system of fair trade and competition, we have added to the prosperity and wealth of these lands, and checked famine and disease. We have put an end to the awful misery of the slave-trade and inter-tribal war, to human sacrifice and the ordeals of the witch-doctor. . . We are endeavouring to teach the native races to conduct their own affairs with justice and humanity, and to educate them alike in letters and in industry (118)."

Civil wars   Lugard recalled conditions in Uganda and Nigeria when he first knew them at the end of the nineteenth century: "In Uganda a triangular civil war was raging – Protestants, Roman Catholics, and Moslems, representing the rival political factions of British, French and Arabs, were murdering each other. Only a short time previously triumphant paganism had burnt Christians at the stake and revelled in holocausts of victims."

He emphasized the change, as he continued: "Today there is an ordered government with its own native parliament. Liberty and Justice have replaced chaos, bloodshed, and war. The wealth of the country steadily increases. The slave-raids and tyranny of the neighbouring Kingdom of Unyoro have given place to similar progress and peace.

Slave raids   "In Nigeria in 1902 slave-raiding armies of 10,000 or 15,000 men laid waste the country, and wiped out its population annually in the quest of slaves. Hundreds of square miles of rich, well-watered land were depopulated . . . Nowhere was there security for life and property. Today the native Emirs vie with each other in the progress of their schools; the native courts administer justice, and themselves have liberated over fifty thousand slaves (119)."

In other parts of Africa, however, European rule brought suffering and misery. In 1885 King Leopold II of the Belgians, frustrated by the insignificance of his tiny kingdom, took the extraordinary step of setting up his own colony in the Congo: "The Congo," he wrote in 1906, "has been, and could have been, nothing but a personal undertaking. There is no more legitimate or respectable right than that of an author over his own work, the fruit of his labour . . . My rights over the Congo are to be shared with none; they are the fruit of my own struggles and expenditure (120)." *The Belgian Congo*

Unfortunately for the Congolese Leopold's bold adventure soon became a tragedy. The rubber trade there was run by ruthless and corrupt administrators, and rumours of ill-treatment and misgovernment soon began to circulate.

In 1903, a British diplomat, Sir Roger Casement, submitted a horrifying report about conditions in King Leopold's colony. Describing a hospital he visited, Casement reported: "When I visited the three mud huts which serve the purpose of the native hospital [in Leopoldville], all of them dilapidated, and two with the thatched roofs almost gone, I found seventeen sleeping sickness patients, male and female, lying about in the utmost dirt. Most of them were lying on the bare ground – several out on the pathway in front of the houses, and one, a woman, had fallen into the fire just prior to my arrival (while in the final, insensible stage of the disease) and had burned herself very badly . . . *Hospital for Africans*

"In somewhat striking contrast to the neglected state of these people, I found, within a couple of hundred yards of them, the government workshops for repairing and fitting the steamers. Here all was brightness, care, order, and activity, and it was impossible not to admire and commend the industry which had created and maintained in constant working order this useful establishment (121)." *A marked contrast*

Later, a Congolese villager described to Casement the system of payment for rubber-picking: "Our village got cloth and a *Rubber picking* 93

Overleaf A European official addresses a village council in the Congo

little salt, but not the people who did the work. Our chiefs ate up the cloth; the workers got nothing. The pay was a fathom of cloth and a little salt for every big basketful, but it was given to the chief, never to the men. It used to take ten days to get the twenty baskets of rubber – we were always in the forest, and then when we were late we were killed. We had to go farther and farther into the forest to find the rubber vines, to go without food, and our women had to give up cultivating the fields and gardens. Then we starved. Wild beasts – the leopards – killed some of us when we were working away in the forest, and others got lost or died from exposure and starvation, and we begged the white men to leave us alone, saying we could get not more rubber, but the white men and their soldiers said: 'Go! You are only beasts yourselves . . .'

"We tried, always going farther into the forest, and when we *Soldiers'* failed and our rubber was short, the soldiers came to our towns *brutalities* and killed us. Many were shot, some had their ears cut off; others tied up with ropes around their necks and bodies and taken away. The white men sometimes at the posts did not know of the bad things the soldiers did to us, but it was the white men who sent the soldiers to punish us for not bringing in enough rubber (122)."

The administration of the Congo was obviously corrupt. In 1908, control of the Congo was transferred to the Belgian government who continued to administer it, until the colony was granted a hurried and premature independence in 1960.

In the French Congo things were no better. An account of *The French* conditions there in 1925 hardly tallies with the idealized picture *Congo* painted by propagandists of imperial rule: "The Census-return gave a total of 4,950,000 natives in 1911 and 2,821,981 in 1921, and, though a more accurate method of taking the census would in part account for the diminution, there can be no doubt that the population declined, and is declining at a rapid rate. Added to the ordinary causes of native depopulation was the influence of several factors local to the Congo – the abuses of the Company-regime, the resultant weakening of the racial stock, sleeping-sickness, and a peculiarly aggravated form of abortion. There is a decline practically everywhere, especially

97

Opposite Cartoon satirizing the European powers' delay in ending the atrocities in the Congo

D

with the coastal tribes. . .

Sleeping
sickness

"Especially ominous is the spread of sleeping-sickness, which has for some years been spreading north past the river tribes and even to the healthier Islamized zone. Of 23,590 natives examined in the Chad region in 1918–1919, for instance, 3,566 died before the next year was out, and lesser instances were not lacking. The war against this scourge started only in 1906 . . . But, even could this specific disease be eradicated or restricted, the greater evil would remain – the disintegration of the native life brought about by an unregulated contact with the worst phases of French civilization (123)."

Tribal life
destroyed

It was this "disintegration of the native life" which was perhaps the most damaging aspect of contact with Europeans. Undeniably, the white man was centuries ahead of the African in technology. But, on the other hand, African society was sophisticated and complex; its highly developed systems of tribal and family relationships had evolved over centuries, as the most suitable to the African way of life. The sudden shock of colonial rule endangered all this.

Effect of
Christianity

Some missionaries recognized Christianity's disturbing impact upon the tribal structure. As one of them admitted, "The Gospel goes dead against everything which distinguishes them as the Amantabele tribe:

(a) It destroys all despotic power, makes men intelligent, thinking and responsible beings who seek for judgement and justice. It takes from the King all Divine power attributed to him and attributes it to God alone. . .

(b) It destroys entirely their military standing. . .

(c) It destroys all polygamy and also that much to be dreaded enemy of all human life and liberty – I mean witchcraft.

"These," he goes on, "are the monuments of this nation in which they glory. To take away Divinity from the king is to make him only a man, and to take away his despotic power is to make him in some measure subject to his subjects. Deprive them of their military standing and how shall they multiply their numbers and add to their already numerous herds of cattle. To take away their plurality of wives is to take away their personal property and to do away with witchcraft is to deprive them of their most effective means of getting rid of all whom they hate and who may stand in their way. These are not matters of faith but of sight and touch and dearer to them than their life's blood (124)."

Africa's ancient tribal organization and way of life gave security to a pre-industrial society. But it was doomed in the face of thrusting European culture.

"I sometimes wonder," wrote a Kenyan observer, "whether *European* the impact of the European mind, its restlessness, its energy, its *restlessness* knowledge, its dynamics, has not created an insoluble problem for the people of Kenya . . . Without the European, the African scene in Kenya could have been tranquil, slow and largely as unconcerned as other countries in Africa.

"But," he continues sadly, "the restless energy of the European *Little material* settler, his insatiable demands for new knowledge, for new *advance* techniques in farming, for better roads, for better administration, for better communications, raised the standard of the whole country beyond that which the indigenous people themselves may well wish to maintain . . . What might have been good enough for a simple immature people, without much technical knowledge or education, was completely unsuited to the type of man who came from the western world intent on making a new country . . . (125)"

The destruction of the old ways of life might have been acceptable if Africans had enjoyed rapid material development. In fact, investment by European countries in Africa was pitifully small; only the mines of southern Africa and the Rhodesias attracted substantial foreign capital.

A Labour Party Report of 1926 was scathing about Britain's *Labour Party* record in East Africa: "The whole organization and administra- *Report* tion of Government is directed . . . towards compelling the African inhabitants to work for European masters, and is based on the absolute subjection of the native population. Labour is recruited and controlled by the Government, and every possible device, including actual conscription, is used to force the natives into the labour market. All land, except what has already been sold to Europeans, belongs to the Crown, and, with the exception of one district in Uganda, Africans have only been allowed to occupy certain limited areas on terms of extreme insecurity. Railways, harbours, mines and factories are owned either by Government or by Europeans.

"What has been the result of a generation of British ownership?

"Parts of East Africa, before Europeans took control, used to export grain. Now it is necessary for the Government to import food into countries which are extraordinarily fertile in every kind of crop. There have been periods of actual famine.

"Diseases, both those which are native to the country and those which have been brought into it by Europeans, have spread with fearful rapidity, and the population in nearly all parts of East Africa is declining (126)."

Threat to wild life   Even the wild life of Africa was endangered and exploited by European sportsmen. One of the most famous nineteenth-century white hunters, Gordon Cummings, describes the slaughter of an elephant: "I followed, loading and firing as fast as could be, sometimes at the head, sometimes behind the shoulder, until the elephant's forequarters were severely punished; notwithstanding which he continued to hold stoutly on, leaving the grass and branches of trees scarlet in his wake, until I began to think he was bullet-proof... Having fired thirty-five rounds with my two-grooved rifle, I opened up on him with the Dutch six-pounder; and when forty bullets had perforated his hide, he began to show symptoms of exhaustion. Poor old fellow... (127)"

White domination   White men were not content that European states should just rule African colonies. They wished to establish white settlements like the "White Dominions" of Canada and Australia. Some visualized an Africa in which white domination was so complete, that the African was no more than an inconvenience or a slave.

Colonel Meinertzhagen described a conversation with the British High Commissioner in Nairobi in 1902: "He envisaged a thriving colony of thousands of Europeans with their families, the whole of the country from the Aberdares and Mount Kenya to the German border [i.e. the border of Tanganyika] divided up into farms; the whole of the Rift Valley cultivated or grazed,

100

The African peoples were not the only victims of European exploitation

and the whole country of Lumbwa, Nandi to Elgon and almost to Baringo under white settlement. He intends to confine the natives to reserves and use them as cheap labour on farms.

"I suggested that the country belonged to Africans and that *Africans* their interests must prevail over the interests of strangers. He *ignored* would not have it . . . I said that some day the African would be educated and armed; that would lead to a clash. Eliot [the High Commissioner] thought that that day was so far distant as not to matter and that by that time the European element would be strong enough to look after themselves; but I am convinced that in the end the Africans will win and that Eliot's policy can lead only to trouble and disappointment (128)."

Men holding such opinions gave the Africans little con- *Condescend-* sideration: "If you read the history of any part of the Negro *ing colonists* population of Africa," said another British administrator, Sir Bartle Frere, "you will find nothing but a dreary recurrence of tribal wars, and an absence of everything which forms a stable government . . . century after century, these tribes go on obeying no law but that of force, and consequently never emerging from the state of barbarism in which we find them at present, and in which they have lived, so far as we know, for a period long anterior to our own era (129)."

If Africa was to evolve, they argued, white rule was essential. *Africa's* "By their own unaided efforts," wrote yet another Englishman, *dependence* "I doubt whether the Negroes would ever advance much above *on Europe* the status of savagery in which they still exist in those parts of Africa where neither European nor Arab civilization has as yet reached them . . . The Negro seems to require the intervention of some superior race before he can be roused to any definite advance from the low stage of human development in which he has contentedly remained for many thousand years (130)."

All that was needed, according to the romanticists, was an influx of young white settlers. Gertrude Page, a novelist, imagined the ideal colonist: "Clever, handsome, debonair, well-read, he demonstrated unintentionally a healthy form of the simple life, absolutely free of asceticism, or any mawkish effeminacy . . . His farming . . . consisted largely of much prowling around with his gun; with occasional intervals of sowing seed, which invariably came up in the most annoying patches, superintending the curing of bacon and ham, and strolling round to yarn with other healthy young demonstrators of the simple life . . . a good, all-round healthy, vigorous colonist . . . (131)"

Another writer was struck by the contrast between the white man and the African: "Nothing could more forcibly illustrate the difference between extremes of racial character than the picture thus conjured up – the European engineer forcing with incredible toil his broad and certain way, stemming rivers, draining marshes, shattering tons of earth and rock; and, on the other hand, the savage, careless of everything but the present, seeking only the readiest path, and content to let a pebble baulk him rather than stoop to lift it (132)."

But life for European settlers in Africa was often very different from the dreams of novelists and propagandists. Particularly in West Africa, Europeans frequently lived in great squalor and discomfort: "We live on the first floor overlooking a garden," wrote a British merchant in Freetown, Sierra Leone: "In this garden . . . exists a pump drawing water from a well. Within a few yards of this well is a cesspool carefully housed over but never emptied. It is a horrible abomination, quantities of chloride of lime thrown into it and strewed about will not drive away the foul stench emitted. Everything thrown into the cesspool is consumed, or it percolates, perhaps to the well . . .

You lower a lantern through the hole and observe a mass of reptiles and foul insects gorging on filth and offal and on each other . . . but unless householders are compelled to pay for and use the good water they stick to the well. Is it any wonder Sierra Leone is the white man's grave? (133)"

Even in East Africa, with its beautifully dry and pleasant climate, life could be very boring for Europeans.

The club was the centre of social activities. "Here as the sun *The club* went down," wrote Lord Cranworth, "assembled the élite from farm and office, from store and counter. Plates of potato chips and monkey nuts garnished the mahogany, and behind it an autocratic Indian marshalled his troupe of smiling natives in their white kanzas. Drinks flowed freely and so did the conversation, of which one could take one's choice of almost any brand. Certainly as the dinner hour approached the babel became louder and the stories taller and even thicker . . .

"Assuredly," he concluded regretfully, "I had some good times in the old Club, and never ceased regretting when the process of evolution demanded something grander and more dignified (134)."

Other entertainments were few, but the British were deter- *Cricket* mined to play some cricket. As early as the 1830s, we are told, a party of Englishmen, "determined to brave the heat, and insult its power, by a game of cricket, with the thermometer probably at 98 degrees in the shade; they selected the scorching plain of the racecourse for the exertions of this exciting sport, and in full exposure to the meridian sun . . . They left the cricket ground, burning with fever voluntarily sought; and after a fortnight only one is said to have been living (135)."

The heat and the boredom of the life of a white settler often *Africitis* caused psychological troubles, as one British District Commissioner complained in his diary. "My wife has Africitis, it is an infectious disease, approximating to 'the hump' of more civilized lands . . . occasionally an attack commences with violent vituperation of shivering natives, succeeded by lethargy and coma. Sometimes one weeps – that is to say Beryl does; more often in my case at least one curses vigorously the Powers that Be . . . the station and all that appertains thereto . . . until

103

An East African club in the 1890s. For whites only, these clubs were the centre of all social activities

frenzy gives place to sudden calm (136)."

Gradual decadence

The effect of African life upon some white immigrants in South Africa was not good; "descendants of settlers, Dutch or English, or Dutch and English, who had sat dreaming too long in one spot, hypnotized by the enormous forbidding spaces and by the unceasing sun into believing that all was well so long as they sat still, said their prayers, and had the natives fetch and carry.

"The men," according to this observer, "lost imperceptibly the vigour of pioneer grandfathers. The women forgot the industrious skill in cooking, sewing and in the management of a small farm that had been their grandmother's dowry. Even marriages became idle affairs of promiscuity. Few men saddled a horse and rode for a wife. So that in two or three generations the illegitimate, the imbecile, and the slightly foolish were many among them; and dark children were not rare (137)."

Household chores

To survive in Africa, Europeans, particularly the women, had to be exceptionally strong and resourceful. "There is little room," wrote an English observer, "for the display of drawing-

104

room graces and accomplishments. The wife in Natal is either a 'help-meet' in the fullest and strongest sense of the term, or a hindrance and drawback to her husband. The colonial wife commonly needs to be, as well as companion and adviser, the instructor of children, the cook, baker, laundress, gardener, farming bailiff and often tailor. For these duties, solid and sterling qualities are required, rather than refinements and elegancies (138)."

The great advantage for white women living in Africa was the ready supply of domestic servants. Like Mrs. Boyd, many European ladies regarded the African as a cheap and rather inefficient drudge: "What the native wants he takes," she complained, "if he is clever enough to do so unobserved . . . Constitutionally lazy, entirely ignorant, inconceivably stupid and completely unambitious . . . Not only have you to supervise all the work out here, but you also need at least a working knowledge of every branch of the science of living, from house-building to boot cleaning . . . garden boys will have to be instructed how to dig and trench, make paths and plant; the cook required to be shown how to make bread and cakes and pastry, how to fry and how to roast. *Servants*

"You've got to know," Mrs. Boyd went on, "how to build dams, work rams, wash and iron clothes, clean silver and polish floors, make beds and shine shoes, mend your car or your cream separator or your mowing machine, even tune a piano . . . **When** you know all this, as well as a hundred other things, you will require in addition the patience to teach them, and then the patience to see they are carried out (139)."

The relationship between the two races is shown clearly in this picture of an African servant in a European household: "Boxer is our general servant indoor and out. More out than in, because Boxer has a mousy-like odour pervading him, in common with his kind, for which he is not to blame, and by which it is easy to discover when he is trying to sneak noiselessly by the window on some private frolic of his own, leaving me and my household work to take care of ourselves . . . *Boxer*

"Boxer may be aged anywhere between ten and twelve . . . his wool set thick and close to his round bullet of a head; his eyeballs are, if such an anomaly can be, whiter than white, and his teeth almost glisten as his wide mouth opens for a broad grin . . .

"Boxing Boxer's ears was a trial to me, I confess, but I came to that at last, and repeated the dose when I once discovered its efficacy. I had been before but a poor thing in his estimation (140)."

Africa's cheap labour, vast resources and a servile population apparently offered paradise to the white man. But, as the twentieth century progressed, it gradually became clear that Africa was no longer a passive continent, helpless before the technology of European conquerors.

The fires of African nationalism were beginning to burn.

A picnic on the Gold Coast, 1890. The natives remain in the background; they are only tolerated as servants

6 Africa Breaks Free

PERHAPS THE greatest benefit Europe gave to Africa was education. The continent was studded with missionary schools similar to the one described by Kenneth Kaunda, the future president of Zambia: "The method of teaching young children in the nineteen-twenties," he writes in his autobiography, "was to gather them under a tree on which was hung a cloth painted with the letters of the alphabet. I well remember sitting for hours under a shady tree chanting *a–e–i–o–u*, then forming the letters with my fingers in the sand. We would smooth out a little area near where we were sitting and the teacher would wander round among the children correcting our letters. Each cloth was called Nsalu, and when we had Nsalu one, two and three, we were promoted to the first class, where we were allowed to use slates (141)."

Future nationalists

These methods may have been crude, but they trained a whole generation of Africans, many of whom continued their studies at foreign universities, or at African institutions like Fourah Bay College in Sierra Leone. It was these men who formed the spearhead of the struggle to free Africa from European domination.

There had always been individual Africans who opposed colonial rule and dreamed of self government. It was only as the twentieth century progressed that this opposition became organized.

Effect of wars

The two World Wars had a profound effect upon the many thousands of Africans who fought in them. A British Commission reported: "The large number of African soldiers

107

A Roman Catholic church school in southern Rhodesia. Education was the beginning of African discontent with the old way of life

returning from service with the Forces, where they had lived under different and better conditions, made for a general communicable state of unrest. Such Africans by reason of their contacts with other peoples including Europeans had developed a political and national consciousness. The fact that they were disappointed at conditions on their return, either from specious promises made before demobilization or a general expectancy of a golden age for heroes, made them the natural focal point for any general movement against authority (142)."

*Soldiers'
dissatisfaction*

Another British report came to the same conclusion: "In the Second World War, in particular, he [the African] was brought into contact with the outside world, and he established a new relationship with men of other races. He returned to civilian life with changed tastes and standards, but soon found that the opportunities for earning a level of income which he had lived up to in the army did not exist (143)."

*Technology
and Africa*

The Report also commented upon the effect of technology in Africa: "The effect of modern technical inventions on the lives of Africans must be mentioned. Most important have been modern means of communication. The train, the bus, the bicycle and telecommunications have broken down the isolation and parochialism of communities and have speeded up the

108

Opposite After the Second World War Africa became more industrialized.
One African looks on as an excavator gets to work

operation of so many of the factors effecting change. The wireless and the press are also powerful influences both for good and ill (144)."

Under the pressures of world wars, western education and economic change, Africans began to organize themselves to claim a say in their future.

The Pan-African Congress of 1919 made some elementary demands about education: "It shall be the right of every native child," the Congress proclaimed, "to learn to read and write his own language, and the language of the trustee nation, at public expense, and to be given technical instruction in some branch of industry. The State shall also educate as large a number of natives as possible in higher technical and cultural training and maintain a corps of native teachers (145)."

Pan-African Congress

The Congress had strong views about Africans' rôle in the state: "The natives of Africa must have the right to participate in the government as fast as their development permits, in conformity with the principle that the government exists for the natives, and not the natives for the government. They shall at once be allowed to participate in local and tribal government, according to ancient usage, and this participation shall gradually extend, as education and experience proceed, to the higher

African participation in government

Kwame Nkrumah, the first Prime Minister of Ghana (the former Gold Coast). Under his leadership, Ghana was the first British African colony to gain its independence

offices of State; to the end, that, in time, Africa be ruled by consent of the Africans . . . (146)"

Soon African leaders began to organize political parties and pressure groups to demand a greater say in government and eventual independence.

Kwame Nkrumah Kwame Nkrumah, who later became the President of Ghana, described how "we managed to collect together some motor vans to which we attached loudspeakers. These, together with the *Accra Evening News*, the *Sekondi Morning Telegraph* and the *Cape Coast Daily Mail* did yeoman service in broadcasting the propaganda of the Party and in keeping alive the spirit of nationalism.

"We were not disturbed by those who labelled us 'verandah boys, hooligans and Communists'; we had succeeded where they had failed. We had succeeded because we had talked with the people and by so doing knew their feelings and grievances. And we had excluded no-one. For, if a national movement is to succeed, every man and woman of goodwill must be allowed to play a part (147)."

The Mau-Mau As late as the 1950s, it seemed that organized and peaceful

Opposite Anglo-French troops landing in Egypt in 1956, in the hope of stopping Nasser nationalizing the Suez Canal

opposition to colonial rule was making little headway. Some of the more militant African tribes, such as the Kikuyu of Kenya, used violence to obtain results. Europeans were killed, farms burned, cattle and crops destroyed. The Kikuyu took a solemn Swahili oath which proclaimed their unity and purpose within the Mau-Mau organization (148):

> *I speak the oath and vow before our God*
> *And by this Betuni oath of our movement*
> *Which is called the movement of fighting*
> *That is I am called on to kill for our soil*
> *If I am called on to shed my blood for it*
> *I shall obey and I shall never surrender*
> > *And if I fail to go*
> > *May this oath kill me,*
> > *May this he-goat kill me,*
> > *May this seven kill me*
> > *May this meat kill me.*

When the process of decolonization eventually began, it was sudden and rapid. Ironically, Egypt, which had witnessed the beginning of European rule in Africa, also saw the beginning of its end. On 26th July, 1956, President Nasser of Egypt ordered the Suez Canal to be nationalized: "The International Company of the Suez Maritime Canal . . . ," he proclaimed, "is hereby nationalized. Its assets and liabilities revert to the State and the councils and committees at present responsible for its administration are dissolved . . .

Suez Canal nationalized

"Payment of . . . compensation will be made when all the assets of the nationalized company have been fully handed over to the State (149)."

British and French resistance

The British and the French, outraged by this action, attempted to retain control of the Canal by force, but world opinion and their economic circumstances forced them to beat a humiliating retreat. Africa had won its first victory against foreign domination.

The Suez affair convinced many Europeans that they had neither the resources nor the will to hang on any longer to unwilling colonies.

"Wind of change"

The English Prime Minister, Harold Macmillan, had also realized the impossibility of opposing the movement towards independence in Africa: "The wind of change," he told a South African audience in a famous speech, "is blowing through this continent. Whether we like it or not, this growth of national consciousness is a political fact. We must all accept it as a fact. Our national policies must take account of it (150)."

Decolonization

In 1957, the rush towards independence began when the former Gold Coast was created an independent state with the ancient name of Ghana. In 1960, General Charles de Gaulle offered independence to all French territories in Africa, and in the same year the Belgians abandoned their huge Congolese empire. Throughout the 1960s territory after territory gained its freedom.

At the U.N.

The new African states soon made themselves felt in the United Nations, which reflected their influence by declaring, in 1962, that: "The subjection of peoples to alien subjugation, domination and exploitation constitutes a denial of fundamental rights, is contrary to the Charter of the United Nations and is an impediment to the promotion of world peace and co-operation (151)." It was clear that the colonial era had ended.

South Africa

In the rush towards African rule, one major area of white dominance remained intact, the Portuguese colonies and the Union of South Africa. In South Africa, the Nationalist Party, dedicated to white supremacy, had grown steadily in strength since the Boer War. In 1948, the Nationalists won a large majority and were free to put their policy of apartheid, or

The newly independent African countries became forceful members of
the United Nations

separate development, into operation.

"The Republic of South Africa," states a South African
Government publication, "has its own special part to play in
human affairs. It bears responsibility for a multi-national
population more complex than any on earth. To meet this
situation it has a clear-cut policy, based on three considerations:

"That the people of South Africa do not comprise one
nation but distinctive White and Black – or Bantu nations.

"That throughout Africa today African peoples are claiming
the right to express their own personality and nationhood.

"That the White nation in South Africa has the same right.
Accordingly, the aims of the New Republic's policy are:

"To give to the White and Bantu peoples in equal degree the
opportunity to maintain and develop the type of social and
political organization best suited to the expression of their own
particular characteristics and aspirations.

"To maintain the position of the White nation in those parts
of South Africa which the European immigrants settled over a

113

period of some 300 years (152)."

Eventually this would lead to a complete separation of the races, and the establishment of white and black areas within the Republic.

Apartheid An African writer described the practical result of such a policy: "Which are these two South Africas, one for Whites and the other for Africans? In Dr. Verwoerd's 'European' territory live six million Africans, one and a half million coloureds (those of mixed descent), half a million Indians, and three million Whites. The total area of South Africa is 472,359 square miles. The area of the 'European' territory is 416,130 square miles. The remainder, some fifty-six thousand square miles, or less than twelve per cent of the total, is the land comprising the 'Bantu homelands.' Here live five million Africans.

Bias towards "The so-called White state is a contiguous land area, con-
whites taining practically all the natural resources and advanced development secured by the labour and skill of all South Africans – the majority of whom, of course, are Africans. This territory includes all the large cities, the seaports, the harbours, the airfields, the areas served well by railways, main roads, power lines, and major irrigation schemes. It contains the enormously rich gold mines, the diamond mines, the coal mines. It includes all the main industries, maintained largely by African labour, in this industrially advanced country. It includes the best and most fertile farmlands.

"The 'Bantu homelands' consist of two hundred and sixty small and separate areas scattered throughout the country. They are South Africa's backwaters, primitive rural slums, soil-eroded and under-developed, lacking power resources and without developed communication systems (153)."

Southern In 1965, the area under white rule in southern Africa was
Rhodesia increased when the Colony of Southern Rhodesia proclaimed its independence from Britain, and set up a régime dominated by the tiny white population:

"Now therefore," the Rhodesian leader Ian Smith declared, "we, the Government of Rhodesia, in humble submission to Almighty God who controls the destinies of nations, conscious

"White" colonies also became restive, and Rhodesia, under her Prime Minister Ian Smith (right), left the British Commonwealth

that the people of Rhodesia have always shown unswerving loyalty and devotion to Her Majesty the Queen and earnestly praying that we and the people of Rhodesia will not be hindered in our determination to continue exercising our undoubted right to demonstrate the same loyalty and devotion, seeking to promote the common good so that the dignity and freedom of all men may be assured, do, by this proclamation, adopt, enact and give to the people of Rhodesia the Constitution annexed hereto.

"God save the Queen (154)."

The independent African countries face enormous problems if they are to survive in the modern world. Africa may be politically free, but her economy is still dominated by foreigners.

Economic problems

"Immense profits have been, and are still being, taken out of Africa," wrote Kwame Nkrumah. "Important mineral deposits in various parts of Africa have attracted foreign capital, which has been used mainly to enrich alien investors... The Anglo-American Corporation of South Africa with its associated diamond combine, besides having a practical monopoly of all the diamonds produced in Africa, and owning many gold and coal mines in South Africa, has a large stake in the Rhodesian copper belt.

115

"Much of the great mineral wealth of Africa, which ought to have been kept in Africa to develop basic industries here, has been systematically shipped away. The process is still going on, even in the independent countries (155)."

Social problems
Another problem facing newly independent states is the lack of a stable middle class, as the African intellectual, Franz Fanon, realized: "In Africa, the countries that come to independence are as unstable as their middle classes or their renovated princes. After a few hesitant steps in the international arena the national middle classes, no longer feeling the threat of the traditional colonial power, suddenly develop great appetites. And as they do not yet have any political experience they think they can conduct political affairs like their business. Perquisites, threats, even despoiling of the victims (156)."

Success in unity?
The future of Africa in the twentieth century will not be easy, but the continent has huge resources and no lack of energy and confidence. Perhaps, as Kwame Nkrumah hoped, the solution lies in unity: "The survival of free Africa, the extending independence of this continent, and the development towards that bright future on which our hopes and endeavours are pinned, depend upon political unity . . .

"The forces that unite us are far greater than the difficulties that divide us at present, and our goal must be the establishment of Africa's dignity, progress and prosperity (157)."

Map of African
Independence

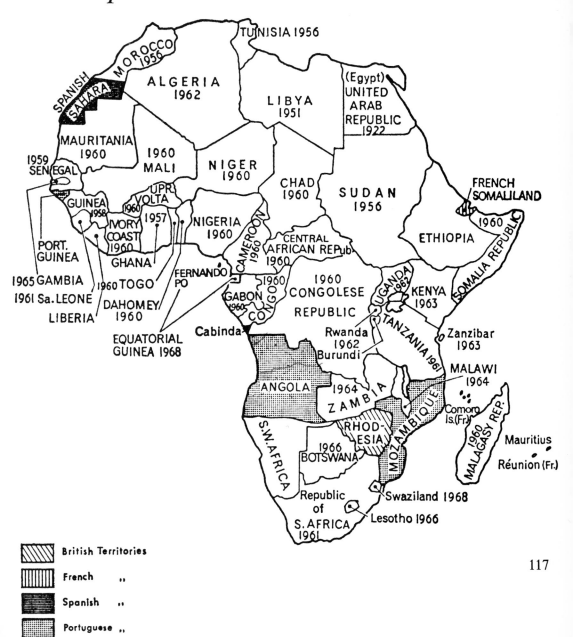

TUNISIA 1956

SPANISH SAHARA

MOROCCO 1956

ALGERIA 1962

LIBYA 1951

(Egypt)
UNITED ARAB REPUBLIC 1922

MAURITANIA 1960

1959 SENEGAL

1960 MALI

NIGER 1960

CHAD 1960

SUDAN 1956

FRENCH SOMALILAND

GUINEA 1958

1960

UPR. VOLTA 1960

1957

NIGERIA 1960

CAMEROON 1960

CENTRAL AFRICAN REPub. 1960

ETHIOPIA

SOMALIA REPUBLIC 1960

PORT. GUINEA

IVORY COAST 1960

GHANA

FERNANDO PO

1960

GABON 1960

1960 CONGOLESE REPUBLIC

UGANDA 1962

KENYA 1963

1965 GAMBIA
1961 Sa. LEONE
LIBERIA

1960 TOGO
DAHOMEY 1960

CONGO

Rwanda 1962
Burundi

TANZANIA 1961

Zanzibar 1963

EQUATORIAL GUINEA 1968

Cabinda

MALAWI 1964

ANGOLA

1964

ZAMBIA

Comoro Is.(Fr.)

MOZAMBIQUE

1960 MALAGASY REP.

S.W. AFRICA

RHOD-ESIA

1966 BOTSWANA

Mauritius

Réunion (Fr.)

Republic of S. AFRICA 1961

Swaziland 1968

Lesotho 1966

Legend:

⧄	British Territories
⦀	French ,,
▬	Spanish ,,
▦	Portuguese ,,
☐	Independent States

Dramatis Personae

BATTUTA, Muhammad Ibn Abdulah Ibn (1304–1377). Arab traveller born in Marrakesh; one of the best sources of information about medieval Africa.

BAKER, Sir Samuel (1821–1893). One of the chief explorers of central Africa; discovered Lake Albert Nyanza in 1864.

BULLER, Sir Redvers (1839–1908). Commanded British army in South Africa at outset of Boer War; disgraced and relieved of his command.

CHAMBLERLAIN, Joseph (1836–1914). British Colonial Secretary 1895–1903 and arch-exponent of Imperialism.

FERRY, Jules (1832–1893). Twice Premier of France; firm believer in French imperial expansion.

KRUGER, Paul (1825–1904). President of the Transvaal during crucial period in Anglo–Boer relations.

LEOPOLD II, King of the Belgians (1835–1909). Founded Congo Free State, which was his private property until 1908.

LIVINGSTONE, David (1813–1862). Perhaps the greatest of nineteenth century missionaries and explorers; lost for many years in the bush until found by Stanley.

LUGARD, Sir Frederick (1858–1945). British proconsul and apologist for colonial rule; dominated Nigerian administration between 1900 and 1919.

MANSA MUSA, Emperor of Mali (1312–1337). One of the greatest monarchs of medieval Africa; extended his kingdom over huge area.

MILNER, Sir Alfred (1854–1925). Governor of Cape Colony after 1897; played large part in events leading to Boer War.

NASSER, Gamal Abdel (1918–1970). Became President of Egypt shortly after officers' coup in 1952. Precipitated crisis by nationalizing Suez Canal in 1956.

NKRUMAH, Kwame (1909–1972). African nationalist and advocate of African unity; first President of Ghana; deposed in coup.

RHODES, Cecil (1853–1902). Determined to extend British Empire in Africa; became premier of Cape Colony in 1890; forced to resign after Jameson raid in 1896.

ROBERTS, Frederick, Earl (1832–1914). Replaced Buller as Commander in Chief in South Africa; became hero of British public after turning the tide of war.

SMITH, Ian Rhodes (Born 1919). First Prime Minister of independent Rhodesia; took Rhodesia out of British control in 1965.

SPEKE, John Hanning (1827–1864). African explorer who established that Lake Victoria is a source of the Nile.

STANLEY, Sir Henry Morton (1841–1904). Made numerous journeys into Africa; in 1871, found Livingstone at Ujiji; helped to establish the Congo Free State.

Table of Dates

1948 Nationalists win control in South Africa.

1956 Britain and France use force against President Nasser.

1957 Gold Coast gains independence.

1960 Harold Macmillan's "Wind of Change" speech. French African territories gain independence. Congolese Republic proclaimed. Nigeria gains independence.

1961 South Africa becomes a Republic.

1962 French leave Algeria.

1965 Ian Smith declares Rhodesian independence.

1967 Nigerian Civil War begins.

Picture Credits

The author and publishers wish to thank the following for their kind permission to reproduce copyright illustrations on the pages mentioned: Keystone Press Agency, 108, 109, 110, 111, 113, 115; the Mansell Collection, *frontispiece*, 17, 19, 34–35, 49, 50, 52–53, 57, 61, 67, 76–77, 82, 89, 96; the Radio Times Hulton Picture Library, 12, 22, 24, 28, 38–39, 43, 46–47, 55, 58–59, 70–71, 73, 74, 81, 90, 94–95, 101, 104, 106. The maps on pages 8, 31, 64 and 117 are reproduced by permission of Andre Deutsch from *The History of Britain in Africa*, by John Hatch, published in 1969. The jacket picture is reproduced by courtesy of Camera Press Ltd.

List of Sources

(1) Sir Philip Mitchell, quoted by J. Gunter, *Inside Africa* (London, 1955)
(2) Quoted by J. H. Breasted, *Ancient Records of Egypt* (Chicago, 1906)
(3) James Bruce, *Travels to Discover the Source of the Blue Nile* (London, 1790)
(4) D. P. Mannix, *Those About to Die* (London, 1960)
(5) Quoted by B. Davidson, *The African Past* (London, 1964)
(6) Leo Africanus, *The History and Description of Africa done into English by John Pory* (Hakluyt Society, 1896)
(7) Quoted by Davidson, *op. cit.*
(8) H. A. R. Gibb, *Ibn Battuta, Travels in Asia and Africa* (London, 1929)
(9) Quoted by Davidson, *op. cit.*
(10) *Ibid*
(11) G. S. P. Freeman-Grenville, *East African Coast, Select Documents* (London, 1962)
(12) J. J. L. Duyvendak, *China's Discovery of Africa* (London, 1949)
(13) Quoted by Davidson, *op. cit.*
(14) E. G. Ravenstein, *A Journal of the First Voyage of Vasco da Gama* (Hakluyt Society, 1898)
(15) *Ibid*
(16) *Ibid*
(17) M. Longworth Dames, *The Book of Duarte Barbosa* (Hakluyt Society, 1918)
(18) *Ibid*
(19) *Ibid*
(20) G. M. Theal, *Records of South-eastern Africa* (London, 1900)
(21) Andrew Sparrman, *A Voyage to the Cape of Good Hope, etc. 1772–1776* (London, 1785)
(22) Freeman-Grenville, *op. cit.*
(23) *Ibid*
(24) Longworth Dames, *op. cit.*
(25) Theal, *op. cit.*
(26) Davidson, *op. cit.*
(27) J. W. Blake, *Europeans in West Africa* (Hakluyt Society, 1942)
(28) Davidson, *op. cit.*
(29) William Bosman, *A New and Accurate Description of Guinea, etc.* (London, 1705)
(30) Richard Jobson, *The Golden Trade* (London, 1623)
(31) Bosman, *op. cit.*
(32) J. Barbot, quoted in A. and J. Churchill, *Collection of Voyages and Travels* (London, 1732)
(33) *Ibid*
(34) *Ibid*
(35) John Lok, quoted by Davidson, *op. cit.*
(36) Richard Brew, quoted by Davidson, *op. cit.*
(37) Bosman, *op. cit.*
(38) Blake, *op. cit.*
(39) C. B. Wadström, *Observations on the Slave Trade, etc.* (London, 1789)
(40) Mungo Park, *Travels in Interior Districts of Africa* (London, 1799)
(41) *Ibid*
(42) Bosman, *op. cit.*
(43) J. Pope-Hennessey, *Sins of the Fathers* (London, 1967)
(44) Ottobah Cuguano, *Thoughts and Sentiments, etc.* (London, 1787)
(45) Pope-Hennessey, *op. cit.*
(46) Davidson, *op. cit.*
(47) *Ibid*
(48) P. Edwards, ed. *Equiano's Travels* (London and New York, 1967)
(49) Wadström, *op. cit.*
(50) Bosman, *op. cit.*
(51) Robert Norris, *Memoirs of the Reign of Bossa Ahadee, King of Dahomey* (London, 1789)
(52) Cuguano, *op. cit.*
(53) J. Hatch, *A History of Britain in Africa* (London, 1969)
(54) Pope-Hennessey, *op. cit.*
(55) Hatch, *op. cit.*
(56) Quoted by R. Lewis and Y. Foy, *The*

British in Africa (London, 1971)

(57) *Ibid*

(58) *Ibid*

(59) Sir S. Baker, *The Albert N'Yanza.* (London, 1898)

(60) R. Lander, *Records of Clapperton's last Expedition* (London, 1829)

(61) D. Livingstone, *Missionary Travels and Researches in South Africa* (London, 1857)

(62) I. Burton, *The Life of Captain Sir Richard F. Burton* (London, 1893)

(63) J. H. Speke, *Journal of the Discovery of the Source of the Nile* (London, 1863)

(64) Lewis and Foy, *op. cit.*

(65) H. Waller, *The Last Journals of David Livingstone in Central Africa* (London, 1874)

(66) Baker, *op. cit.*

(67) Bruce, *op. cit.*

(68) Baker, *op. cit.*

(69) Quoted by H. Cairns, *Prelude to Imperialism* (London, 1965)

(70) H. M. Stanley, *How I found Livingstone in Central Africa* (London, 1872)

(71) Sir F. Lugard, *The Rise of our East African Empire* (Edinburgh and London, 1893)

(72) *Ibid*

(73) Baker, *op. cit.*

(74) W. F. Moneypenny and G. E. Buckle, *Life of Benjamin Disraeli* (London, 1910–20)

(75) Quoted by W. L. Langer, *European Alliances and Alignments* (New York, 1964)

(76) J. Seeley, *The Expansion of England* (London, 1883)

(77) Quoted by Langer, *op. cit.*

(78) Quoted by S. H. Roberts, *French Colonial Policy* (London, 1929)

(79) *Ibid*

(80) Joseph Chamberlain, *Foreign and Colonial Speeches* (London, 1897)

(81) W. Bagehot, *Physics and Politics* (New York, 1902)

(82) Quoted in W. Langer, *The Diplomacy of Imperialism* (New York, 1950)

(83) *Ibid*

(84) *Ibid*

(85) Sir Alfred Milner, *Africa in Egypt* (London, 1902)

(86) Langer, *Diplomacy of Imperialism*

(87) Hansard, Ser: IV, Vol. XXXII, pp. 388–406

(88) Lewis and Foy, *op. cit.*

(89) W. Churchill, *The River War* (London, 1898)

(90) *Ibid*

(91) Livingstone, *op. cit.*

(92) Quoted by B. Roberts, *Cecil Rhodes and the Princess* (London, 1969)

(93) Langer, *Diplomacy of Imperialism*

(94) Alfred Austin, *Jameson's Raid*

(95) Die Grosse Politik XI, No. 2610

(96) Quoted by R. Robinson, J. Gallagher and A. Denny, *Africa and the Victorians* (London, 1965)

(97) J. L. Garvin and J. Amery, *The Life of Joseph Chamberlain* (London, 1932–1951)

(98) Quoted by R. Kruger, *Goodbye, Dolly Grey* (London, 1959)

(99) Garvin and Amery, *op. cit.*

(100) *The Times History of the War in South Africa* (London, 1906)

(101) Rudyard Kipling, "Bobs"

(102) *The Times,* 21st May, 1900, quoted by B. Gardner, *Mafeking* (London, 1966)

(103) Quoted by Gardner, *op. cit.*

(104) Quoted by Kruger, *op. cit.*

(105) *The Cape Gazette,* quoted by G. H. L. Le May, *British Supremacy in South Africa* (Oxford, 1965)

(106) Le May, *op. cit.*

(107) Anon. *Memoirs of a Man of No Importance* (Frome, 1898)

(108) J. A. Spender, *Life of Sir Henry Campbell-Bannerman* (London, 1923)

(109) George Bernard Shaw, *Man of Destiny*

(110) Lord Curzon, speech, 11th December, 1907

(111) Rudyard Kipling, "The White Man's Burden"

(112) E. Picard, quoted by R. Slade, *King Leopold's Congo*

(113) R. M. Ballantyne, *Six Months at the Cape* (London, 1879)

(114) Sir Frederick Lugard, *The Dual Mandate in British Tropical Africa* (Edinburgh, 1926)

(115) Quoted by Langer, *Diplomacy of Imperialism*

(116) Quoted by T. W. Wallbank, *Documents on Modern Africa* (New York, 1942)

(117) Quoted by B. Porter, *Critics of Empire* (London, 1968)

(118) Lugard, *op. cit.*

(119) *Ibid*

(120) Quoted by Slade, *op. cit.*

(121) Quoted by P. Singleton-Gates and M. Girodias, *The Black Diaries*

(122) *Ibid*

(123) S. Roberts, *op. cit.*

(124) Quoted by Cairns, *op. cit.*

(125) M. Blundell, *So Rough a Wind: Kenya Memoirs* (London, 1964)

(126) *British Imperialism in East Africa* (Labour Research Department, London, 1926)

(127) Lewis and Foy, *op. cit.*

(128) Colonel R. Meinertzhagen, *Kenya Diary. 1902–1906* (London, 1957)

(129) Quoted by Cairns, *op. cit.*

(130) *Ibid*

(131) Quoted by Lewis and Foy, *op. cit.*

(132) H. L. Duff, *Nyasaland under the Foreign Office* (London, 1903)

(133) J. Whitford, *Trading Life in Western and Central Africa* (London, 1967)

(134) Lord B. Cranworth, *A Colony in the Making* (London, 1912)

(135) Quoted by Lewis and Foy, *op. cit.*

(136) C. Gouldsburg, *An African Year* (London, 1912)

(137) Quoted by Lewis and Foy, *op. cit.*

(138) *Ibid*

(139) Joyce Boyd, *My Farm in Lion Country* (London, 1933)

(140) Quoted by Lewis and Foy, *op. cit.*

(141) Kenneth D. Kaunda, *Zambia Shall be Free: An Autobiography* (London, 1962)

(142) Quoted by T. W. Wallbank, *op. cit.*

(143) *Ibid*

(144) *Ibid*

(145) Quoted by W. Burghardt Du Bois, *The World and Africa* (New York, 1947)

(146) *Ibid*

(147) K. Nkrumah, *Ghana: An Autobiography* (London, 1957)

(148) Quoted by J. M. Karuiki, *Mau Mau Detainee* (Oxford. 1963)

(149) *Annual Register of World Events* (London, 1957)

(150) Harold Macmillan, speech, 1960

(151) Quoted by Wallbank, *op. cit.*

(152) *Ibid*

(153) G. Mbeki, *South Africa: the Peasants' Revolt*

(154) Ian Smith, broadcast of 11th November, 1965

(156) K. Nkrumah, *Africa Must Unite* (London, 1963)

(156) F. Fanon, *Toward the African Revolution* (New York, 1967)

(157) Nkrumah, *Africa Must Unite, op. cit.*

Glossary

APARTHEID A system of social, economic and political separation of the races, at present practiced in South Africa.

ASTROLABE An instrument which aided navigation by allowing exact measurement of the stars.

CANKY An African alcoholic drink.

CORNET A junior cavalry officer.

CRAAL (Kraal) A collection of huts surrounded by a fence or stockade.

EMIR An Arab word, meaning prince, governor or commander.

HASSEGAI (Assegai) A slender throwing spear used by South African tribes.

HIEROGLYPHICS A type of writing using small symbolic pictures. First found on ancient Egyptian monuments.

KAFIR (Kaffir) From the Arab word meaning "infidel". Used in South Africa to describe all black tribesmen.

LANTEEN SAIL A triangular sail which could be adjusted to take full advantage of changing winds.

LATICES Trees containing latex, used for making rubber.

MACKRONS Slaves who were deemed unfit to make the Atlantic crossing.

ORYX A kind of African deer, or antelope.

PALANQUIN A covered litter carried on long poles by bearers.

PLANTAIN A plant similar to the banana, which forms a staple food in tropical countries.

RAMADHAN The ninth month of the Muslim year, during which all Muslims must fast in the daylight hours.

SLEEPING SICKNESS An African disease with symptoms of increasing lethargy and dullness.

SPAN The distance from the tip of the little finger to the end of the thumb.

VELD (Veldt) The open grasslands of South Africa.

VERANDAH A cool gallery, open at the sides, but protected from the sun by a roof.

VIZIR (Vizier) A high official or minister of state.

Further Reading

H. A. C. Cairns, *Prelude to Imperialism* (London, Routledge, 1965)

P. D. Curtin, *The Image of Africa* (Wisconsin, 1964)

B. Davidson, *The African Past* (London, Gollancz, 1961)

P. Edwards (ed), *Equiano's Travels* (London, Heinemann, 1967)

D. K. Fieldhouse, *The Colonial Empires* (London, Weidenfeld, 1966)

E. Grierson, *The Imperial Dream* (London, Collins, 1972)

J. Hatch, *A History of Postwar Africa* (London, Deutsch, 1966)

J. Hatch, *The History of Britain in Africa* (London, Deutsch, 1969)

D. Judd, *The Victorian Empire* (London, Weidenfeld, 1970)

R. Oliver & J. D. Fage, *A Short History of Africa* (London, Penguin, 1970)

R. Robinson & J. Gallagher, *Africa and the Victorians* (London, MacMillan, 1961)

Index

127